FACILITY MANAGERS & ENGINEERING DEPARTMENT
OPERATIONS MANUAL

Pages 1–75 Admin
Pages 75-115 Programs
Pages 115-134 Systems
Pages 134-165 General
Pages 165-189 Additional Info

ADMINISTRATION

PROPERTY OPERATIONS POLICIES AND PROCEDURES

PURPOSE: To establish budget preparation and control guidelines for Engineering Department expenditures

POLICY: The Chief Engineer is to implement Budget Control guidelines in accordance with the following procedures as well as with any policies issued by the Accounting Department.

STANDARDS:
1. The Chief Engineer **will prepare** the Engineering Department Fiscal Budget.
2. The monthly budget is to be forecasted and variances explained where required.
3. The Chief Engineer **will maintain an expense tracking system in order to control the monthly budget.**
4.
5. Monthly utility accruals are to be **developed** by the Chief Engineer.
6. All expenses will be coded to the appropriate Engineering account number by the Chief Engineer. Any expenses will be charged to the Engineering budget **must be approved** by the Chief Engineering.

PROCEDURE:
1. The Annual Energy and Repair and Maintenance Fiscal Budgets **are to be developed** by the Chief Engineers.
2. The following information is to be obtained:

   • Marketing plan
   • Energy and R&M Chart of Accounts
   • Energy and R&M budget spreadsheet forms
   • Prior year and year-to-date actual budget history
   • Projected occupancy and food covers
   · Energy Consumption Report
   • Anticipated utility rate increase
   • Annual service contract expenses
   • Projected cost of parts and materials needed to maintain in the property
   • Anticipated cost of **R&M** pr objects
   · Inhouse labour rates plus budgeted increases

3. The projected budget expense for each account is to be **spread** throughout the twelve month period, using the data above, and then submitted to **Accounting Department** for the General Manager's approval.

4. The Chief Engineer is to develop a workable control mechanism whereby potential red flag budget items are identified as they occur and are to be communicated to the **General Manager and Controller** on a weekly basis. (See Figure I as an example of a tracking format. This can be used, or a detailed breakdown of each account can be set-up).

5. A monthly 30-60-90 day forecast is to be developed, explaining in detail any anticipated variance to the budgeted amounts. The forecast if to be submitted to the **Accounting Department.**

6. Utility accruals are to be **developed monthly** by the Chief Engineer. Accruals are determined by calculating the actual utility consumption to date and projecting the consumption for the remaining period. The present utility average rates are multiplied by the projected consumption to obtain the accrual amounts.

7. All monthly expenses are to be verified against the **Financial Reporting System** (FRS) which is to be submitted to the Chief Engineer for review. Errors noted are to be corrected by the Accounting Department the following month.

Note:
Energy and R&M Chart of Account code numbers are to be obtained from the Controller's Office.

8. The Chief Engineer is to code any expense charged to the Engineering Department by the appropriate account number, which is based on the Energy and R&M Chart of Account code numbers.

Note:
The M-T-D General Ledger Distribution List can be used for specific verification information.

9. **Any expense** charged to Engineering is to be reviewed and **approved** by the Chief Engineer prior to posting by the Controller's Department.

10. **No** outside contractors, repairmen, service representatives or parts and materials are to be contracted and/or ordered **by** any department without prior knowledge and approval by the Chief Engineer.

PROPERTY OPERATIONS POLICIES AND PROCEDURES

PURPOSE: To control the Engineering Department inventories and ensure availability of critical parts and supplies.

POLICY: The Chief Engineer will ensure that Department parts and supplies are purchased and controlled.

STANDARDS:
1. All parts and supplies will be stored in secure areas.
2. A minimum par stock of critical parts and supplies will be established and maintained.
3. It is the responsibility of the Chief Engineer, or his designee, to control, and issue inventory.
4. No spare parts or supplies are to be removed from the property.

PROCEDURES
1. A secure storage area must be provided in the maintenance shop for spare parts and supplies. A secure area consists of a lockable room, cage or storage cabinet.
2. Shelving or bins should be used for parts and supplies with in the storage area (s) to provide uniformity and organization. All bins/shelving will be labeled with appropriate identification. The area (s) must be orderly at all times.
3. Access to spare parts and supplies must be restricted to the Engineering Department employees only and these areas are to be locked at all times.
4. A minimum stock or critical parts and supplies that must be on hand for daily operation should be established. Availability and vendor delivery times will be the determining factors in establishing minimum par stocks. Excess inventories are to be avoided whenever possible.
5. Written inventories are to be maintained to identify vendors, pricing, parts numbers, descriptions and maximum and minimum quantities, etc.
6. A parts and supplies inventory is to be conducted regularly, to ensure availability when needed.
7. All Engineering Department employees will be held responsible for maintaining adequate inventories by informing the Chief Engineer or his designee when parts/supplies are getting low.

8. Spare parts and/or supplies are the property of the hotel and **are never to be removed** from the property.

9. Parts and supplies are to be purchased through vendors with whom Hospitality Hotels & Resorts has purchasing agreements where applicable.

10. When selecting vendors, delivery by the vendor is to be considered so as to minimize sending personnel off-property.

11. If the department has a personal computer or access, to one, it is recommended that the parts inventory be computerized.

PROPERTY OPERATIONS POLICIES AND PROCEDURES

PURPOSE:		To provide a system of controlling Property Operations expenses **not directly related to repairs and maintenance.**
POLICY:		The Chief Engineer is to implement Budget Control guidelines in accordance with the following procedures as well as with any policies issued by the Accounting Department.
STANDARDS:	1.	Any project that is expensed to R & M must be initiated through the R & M Project Request procedure.
	2.	The Controllers Department will designate **R & M project account funding.**
	3.	The General Manager must approve any R & M project request.
PROCEDURE:	1.	An R & **M** Project Request Form, as in **Figure 1**, is to be completed when any department requests maintenance services for work which is not repair and maintenance of the existing facility.
	2.	The department head is responsible for completing the top portion of the R & **M** Project Request Form; providing as much detail as possible. Purpose and justification for the project request must be stated clearly and the estimated cost determined.
	3.	The department head must obtain appropriate **Executive Committee member** approval for the concept.
	4.	The Executive Committee member must then obtain the General Manager's signature for concept approval.
	5.	Upon approval of the concept, the Chief Engineer is to determine material, labour and (if necessary) contractor costs. The Chief Engineer then reviews the project with the department head for accuracy and additional information, if required.
	6.	When the cost has been determined, the **Accounting Department** is to designate the appropriate account funding and the R & M Project Request is to be signed by the Hotel Controller.
	7.	Upon completion of the above steps, **final approval** of the request is to be obtained from the General Manager.
	8.	The approved project is then scheduled for completion by the Chief Engineer.

| Subject | R & M PROJECTREQUEST | Section: | ADMINISTRATION | Number 1.3 | Page 2 of 2 |

Figure 1.- R & M PROJECTREQUEST

TO BE COMPLETED BY REQUESTING DEPARTMENT

FROM _____ DATE: _____

DEPARTMENT

PURPOSE OR FUNCTION OF PROJECT:

PROJECT DESCRIPTION: SIZE, SHAPE, TYPE OF FINISH, COLOUR QUANTITY, ETC ,. PROVIDE SKETCH OR ADDITIONAL INFORMATION ON BACK OF THIS FORM.

_____
_____
_____
_____
_____

SPECIFIC AREA: _____ ESTIMATED COST: _____

PERMANENT OR TEMPORARY PROJECT: _____

EXECUTIVE COMMITTEE MEMBER APPROVAL: _____ DATE: _____

GENERAL MANAGER CONCEPT APPROVAL _____ DATE: _____

TO BE COMPLETED BY ENGINEERING DEPARTMENT

PARTS & MATERIAL COST _____ LABOUR COST _____

ESTIMATED HOURS _____ OUTSIDE CONTRACT COST _____

TOTAL COST - - - - - - - - - - - - - **TO BE COMPLETED BY HOTEL CONTROLLER**

TO BE FUNDED FROM _____

DATE: _____

T___ **BE COMPLETED BY EXECUTIVE OFFICE**   CONTROLLER APPROVAL
APPROVED BY _____   DATE _____

GENERAL MANAGER

RETURN TO CHIEF ENGINEER

8

PROPERTY OPERATIONS POLICIES AND PROCEDURES

Subject:	ENERGY CONSUMPTION ANALYSIS Section: ADMINISTRATION
PURPOSE:	To provide a comprehensive means to monitor and control each property utility consumption.
POLICY:	The Chief Engineer is responsible for monitoring the property's energy consumption and maintain the HELP file up to date at all times. |//

STANDARDS:

1. The Chief Engineer is to complete the weekly utility log (HLP.01).
2. The Chief Engineer is to complete and distribute the controller's monthly summary (HLP.02).
3. The Chief Engineer is to complete and submit to Divisional/Regional Office the monthly summary (HLP.03).
4. The Chief Engineer is to complete yearly the ENERGY TARGET (HLP.04) and the justification of target (HLP.05).
5. The Chief Engineer will maintain the HLP file.

PROCEDURES

1. The Chief Engineer is to complete the weekly utility log (form HLP.01) on a timely basis. All the data entered in the weekly utility log must originate from the shifts report.

    a. KWH is the row where you log the daily electricity consumption. At the end of the week calculate the total for the week and enter in the total/average column.

    b. MAX.DEMAND is used if the power company charges for max demand. Enter the daily figures from the meters. In the total/average column enter the highest value reached during the week.

    c. POWER FACTOR (COS) can be a penalizing factor on the electricity bill. Calculate the power on a daily basis and enter the average for the week in the total average column.

    d. LOAD FACTOR shall be calculated on a daily basis. Enter the weekly average in the total/average column.

    e. CHILLER - chiller consumption can reach very high levels in some areas and period. 1r submeters are installed on the chiller circuits enter kwH readings on a daily basis and the weekly total in the total/average column.

f. OIL consumption in liters shall be entered daily. Use tank meters or supply lines meters. The weekly total is entered in the total/average column.

g. STEAM is used for recording operating hours of steam boilers or meter readings from steam/hot water supply.

h. KWH is used to record consumption of kitchen water heaters.

i. OWH is used for recording the total daily water consumption in cubic meter.

j. CITY WATER is used for recording the total daily water consumption in cubic meter.

k. SEWAGE is used to record sewer flow in properties charged for effluent in cubic meter.

l. COOLING TOWERS is used to monitor the make up water consumption and the operation of chemical dosing.

m. SWIMMING POOL is used to monitor the overflow and evaporation of the pool in cubic meter.

n. HOT WATER is used to monitor the hot water consumption in cubic meter.

o. DRY BULB MIN is used in properties where it is impossible to obtain the 24 hours mean temperatures.

p. **DRY BULB MAX** is used with the dry bulb min to calculate the degree days.

q. **AIR MEAN TEMPERATURE** is the 24 hours daily average mean temperature from the weather bureau used to calculate the degree days.

r. **OCCUPANCY**. Enter daily the figure obtained from the Financial Controller.

s. CDD is the calculated cooling degree days calculated in degrees Celsius with a base of 18.3°C.

t. HDD is the calculated heating degree days calculated in degree Celsius with a base of 18.3°C.

u. REMARKS can be used to record miscellaneous information such as Hospitality Hotels & Resorts closing dates, swimming pool refill after cleaning etc.

2. The Chief Engineer is to complete monthly the CONTROLLERS MONTHLY SUMMARY (HLP.02) no later than the Hospitality Hotels & Resorts closing date. All costs in the report must be in local currencies.

3. The Chief Engineer is to complete and submit monthly to Divisional/Regional Office the **MONTHLY SUMMARY** (HLP.03)

Great care should be taken to submit reports on time and with accurate figures. The reported figures will be input for the divisional/regional reports where the performance factor is calculated for each hotel.

REGIONAL MONTHLY SUMMARY (HLP.03) is a report of monthly consumption and expenses to the divisional/regional Engineer. The contents of the various cells is described hereunder:

1. **HOTEL** is the name of the property.

2. **Hospitality HOTELS & RESORTS PERIOD** is the name of the Hospitality Hotels & Resorts month covered in the report. Then Hospitality Hotels & Resorts calendar can be obtained from the Financial Controller.

3. **AVAILABLE ROOMS** is the total number of room nights available in the property. The figure can be obtained from the Financial Controller.

4. **DATE** is the date when the report is completed, usually the closing date of the Hospitality Hotels & Resorts month.

5. **EXCHANGE RATE** is the monthly average exchange rate between the local currency and the US$. The figure can be obtained from the Financial Controller.

6. HOTEL AREA is the hotel area in square meters. However, areas which are not heated, ventilated or air conditioned are not to be included. Parking garages which only have exhaust are not to be included.

7. FUEL OIL is the consumption and cost of fuel oil.

    The first two columns are the actual figures for the current month. Consumption is to be entered in GJ and cost in local currency.

    The next two columns are a running total covering consumption and cost from January to date.

    Column 5 and 6 are the target for the month entered in GJ and local currency.

    The last two columns are a running total covering the target and cost from January to date.

8. GAS is the consumption and cost of gas. Consumption of gas used only for heating purpose is to be entered. Consumption of gas used for cooking is not to be entered. The figures shall be entered as described in 7 FUEL OIL.

9. **STEAM/HOT WATER** is the consumption of steam or hot water if purchased.

10. **ELECTRICITY** is the consumption and the cost of electricity purchased by the property.

11. **TOTAL** is the total of all the above.

12. **HOO** is the row for heating degree days. The first two columns are for the month and year to date actual values. The last two columns are for the predicted monthly and year to date values.

13. **COD** is the row for cooling degree days. The figures shall be entered as in HOD.

14. **OCCUPANCY %** is the hotel occupancy measured in percentage of available rooms for the period. These figures can be obtained from the WEEKLY UTILITY LOG (HLP.0 1) or from the Financial Controller.

15. **COVERS** is the row to enter the total number of covers served in the restaurant during the period.

16. **LAUNDRY PIECES** is the row to enter the total laundry pieces processed in the property during the period. These figures can be obtained from the Housekeeper or the Financial Controller.

17. **WATER** is the row for consumption and cost of water purchased by the property. The figures shall be entered as described in 7 FUEL OIL.

18. **BUDGET HLP** are the heat, light and power actual costs for the current month and year to date. The last two columns are the Budget or Target figures. You will receive monthly the P&I statement from the controller to verify your figures,

19. **BUDGET R&M** are the figures for the repair and maintenance costs. The figure shall be entered as in 18 BUDGET HLP.

20. **REMARKS** is a section to enter justifications or unusual events which could have affected the figures.

21. **STAFF** is the row to enter the total number of staff working in the HLP and R&M sections.

22. **CHIEF ENGINEER** is the row to enter name and signature of the Chief Engineer in charg_e .

4. The Chief Engineer is to complete yearly in December the **ENERGY TARGET (HLP.04)** for the coming year,

5. The Chief Engineer is to complete yearly in December the JUSTIFICATION OF TARGET (HLP .05). This is to be submitted to the Divisional /Regional Office with the ENERGY TARGET to detail and justify energy conservation programs and describe the calculation behind the conservation program.

Subject:	Section:	Number: 1.4
ENERGY CONSUMPTION ANALYSIS	ADMINISTRATION	

6. The Chief Engineer will maintain an updated file which is comprised of the following subdivisions:

   1. Weekly Utility Log (HLP.01)
   2. Controllers Monthly Summary (HLP.02)
   03- SMC Monthly Summary (HLP.03)]
   4. Energy Target (HLP.04)
   5. Justification of Target (HLP.05)
   06- General Site Data (HLP.06)
   07- Electrical Summary (From SMC)
   08- Fuel Oil Summary (From SMC)
   09- Gas Summary (From SMC)
   10- Steam Summary (From SMC)
   11- Total Energy Summary (From SMC)
   12- HLP Budget
   13 Energy Bills
   14 Water Bills
   15 Energy Contracts
   16- Best Fit Line
   17- Weather Data

7. These hotels with personal computer will use the software developed by the Divisional Office for report preparation.

Subject:				Section			Number: 1.4		Page 6 of 10
ENERGY CONSUMPTION ANALYSIS				ADMINISTRATION					
									HLP-01

WEEKLY UTILITY LOG			YEAR			Week No.		

Date								This week	Prev. year
Day	Mon	Tue	Wed	Thu	Fri	Sat	Sun	Total/avr	Total avr.
Kwh									
Max Demand									
Power Factor									
Load Factor									
Chiller (Kwh)									

Oil (liters)									
Steam (kgs)									
KWH									
DWH (m3)									

Subject: ENERGY CONSUMPTION ANALYSIS									Section: ADMINISTRATION	Number: 1.4	
City Water (m3)											
Sewage (m3)											
Cooling Tower (m3)											
Swimmh19Pool (m3)											
Hot Water (m3)											
Dry Bulb Min (°C)											
Dry Bulb Max (°C)											
Avr Mean Temp (·C)											
Occupancy											
Covers											
C OD (·C)											
HOD (·C)											

Remarks

Subject:					Section		Number: 1.4	Page 7 of 10
ENERGY CONSUMPTION ANALYSIS					ADMINISTRATION			
								HLP -0 2
CONTROLLERS MONTHLY SUMMARY						Period		

Electricity	Hotel		Shop 1	Shop 2	Shop3			
Consumption KWH								
Cost								

Water
Consumption capm
Cost

Fuel Oil
Consumption ltrs
Cost

_____

Consumption
Cost

_____

Consumption
Cost
Remarks

_____

Chief Engineer

This report must be submitted to Co11 Troller 11ot later than each Hospitality Hotels & Resorts closing date

Subject	Section	Number: 1.4	
ENERGY CONSUMPTION ANALYSIS	ADMINISTRATION		

HLP-03

REGIONAL MONTHLY SUMMARY

1 Hotel			4 Title	
2 ITT Period			5 Exertint ge R111e	
3 Available Rooms			6 Hote 1 ict1 agr m	

		ACTUAL			TARGET	

	Unit	Cost	Unit	Cost	Unit	Cost	Unit	Cost
7 Fuelol GJ								
8 Gas GJ								
9 Steam/Hotwater GJ								
10 Electricity GJ								
11 Total GJ								

12 HOD

13 COD

14 Occupic						
15 Covers						
16 Laundry Pieces						

17 Water cubic m

18 Budget HLP

19 Budget R&M

	HLP	R&M		
21 Staff			Chief Engineer	

This report must be submitted to SMC no later th11m the first workingbuy fellowsh01111 Wood Hotels I&R report closing of the

Subject: ENERGY CONSUMPTION ANALYSIS		Section: ADMINISTRATION				Number: 1.4		Page 9 of 10
								10.P-04
ENERGY TARGET		Electr					Heating degree days	Cooling degree days
JANUARY								
Tell goQt J								
FEBRUARY								
Tell goQt J								
MARCH								
Tell goQt J								
APRIL								
T R goQt J								
MAY								
Tell goQt J								
JUNE								
Target J								
JULY								
Target J								
AUGUST								
Target J								
SEPTEMBER								
Target J								
OCTOBER								
Tell goQt J								
NOVEMBER								
Tell goQt J								
DECEMBER								
Target J								
TOTAL								
Target J								

Date _____   Chief Engineer _____

NOTE: each month represent a Hospitality Hotels & Resorts calendar month. This report must be submitted together with target justification HL P-05

Subject	Section	Number: 1.4	Page 10 of 10
ENERGY CONSUMPTION ANALYSIS	ADMINISTRATION		

HLP-05

JUSTIFICATION OF TARGET	Hotel	Year

Which area have you considered for energy conservation ?

_____
_____
_____
_____
_____

Why have you chosen these areas?

_____
_____
_____
_____
_____

Area 1		Energy as % of total	
Area 2		Energy as % of total	
Area 3		Energy as % of total	

List here further details and calculations why you want to introduce above conservation program

_____
_____
_____
_____
_____
_____
_____

Use additional paper if 11ce

PROPERTY OPERATIONS POLICIES AND PROCEDURES

Subject:	EXHIBIT SERVICE	Section: ADMINISTRATION
PURPOSE:	To provide special services and utility requirements for exhibitions, groups, meeting planners, vendors or individuals and ensure that charges for such are documented.	
POLICY:	The Chief Engineer will implement and monitor the Exhibit Service procedure.	
STANDARDS:	1. An Exhibit Service form is to be developed by the Chief Engineer.	
	2. It is the responsibility of the sales, property and convention services to ensure the Exhibit Service form is completed and forwarded to the chief Engineer at the earliest possible time.	
	3. The Chief Engineer will schedule the exhibit service set ups based on the completed Exhibit Service forms.	
	4. A 25 percent late charge will be assessed to those clients which request additional services at the last minute, except for banquets.	
	5. Engineering Department labour associated with exhibit services will be recovered to budget.	
PROCEDURES	1. The Chief Engineer will develop an Exhibit Service Form tailored to the hotel's specific needs. See Figure 1 for example form.	
	2. A competitive price review of local hotels is to be conducted at least annually, for services provided and the form updated accordingly.	
	3. Sales, Catering and Convention Services are to use this form exclusively and will review in detail the available services and associated costs with the client. They are to complete the form and distribute to Engineering, Accounting and the Customer.	
	4. In the event the exhibit costs are waived, the form must still be completed in order for the Engineering Department to provide the requested client services.	
	5. The waiving of any exhibit service charges, whether for business reasons or charitable events, must be approved by the General Manager, in addition to the Director of Sales and Marketing or the Director of Food and Beverage. A copy of the waiver approval is to be sent to the Controller's office and the Chief Engineer.	
	6. Timely completion and submission of the form to the Engineering Department is necessary; 10 days prior is recommended. This will promote guest satisfaction by ensuring that the Department has adequate time to prepare for the function.	

PROPERTY OPERATIONS POLICIES AND PROCEDURES

7. The Engineering Department will develop by convention, group, or persons name a list of those clients who require services so that they can be properly scheduled.

8. The Chief Engineer or designee is responsible to ensure that each client has received the agreed upon services and only those in which payment has been made.

9. For Exhibitors requesting additional services at the last minute during a set up, an additional exhibit services form must be completed and a late charge of 25% over regular rates shall be applied. It is the responsibility of the Convention Services Department to update the form and distribute.

10. Due to the short term nature of most banquet business, the 25 percent late charges are to be waived.

11. Labour associated with exhibit services, both straight and overtime rates, including benefits, are chargeable to the client. The actual payroll costs are to be recovered to the Engineering Department budget.

12. At the same time in which the Exhibit Service form is completed, the customer is also to be issued the following information:

    •Fire Safety Policies for Exhibitions (Hospitality Hotels & Resorts or local).

    ·Exhibitor rules such as: forbidding items to be affixed to walls or ceilings, all electrical equipment to be properly grounded, etc.

Cont... of Page 3 of 3

120/208V(3 Ph)1 e)			
01.1,undy Pedic 11ulu d Circuits		Price	To 111
20 AMP		$ 60.00	
	30 AMP	$ 80.00	
40 AMP		$ 100.00	
	50 AMP	$ 120.00	
60 AMP		$ 140.00	
100 A/AP		$ 250.00	
150 A/AP		$ 350.00	
200 A/AP		$ 450.00	

GENERAL CONDITIONS

Electrical Services

Rates quoted for connections cover bring ing o f service to the booth. Should it be necessary to run lines into booth for hooking/convention services manager. Service will be installed on a time a11d material basis. Rates for electrician 11s $ 35.00 per hour from 8:00 AM. on weekdays. Time a1l d one half will prevails after 4:30 P.M. on weekdays. Saturdays, Sul1days, and holidays ($ 52.50 per hour).

QUANTITY	OTHER SERVICES		PRICE
	Ha119 Brow 00 (1). aw	) * * * * *	
	TV (lg. W1 Flux CN lig))	111 _ 111	
	Uor(1)(1)20 L lg'()		
	Ua 11119 Oscil.....Cb. 1901	,, * * ,*,	
	3 15(0)(1)1 (c)E)D)Gen'(en	5* * * * *	
	[Cabviers (AH CONERAL CO 1v, 01 00 NB)	)) * * * * *	
	LA 111R |1H |GENERAL COV0N 0N)(5)		

NOTE: assumes 110 liability failure of electrical sources located
for at the hotel are suitable for any particular purpose.

1. ACCOUNTING COPY - WHITE
2. ENGINEERING COPY - YELLOW
3. CUSTOMER COPY - PINK
4. CONVENTION SERVICE COPY - GOLDENROD

ALL CHARGES SUBJECT TO 8.2 % TAX

PROPERTY OPERATIONS POLICIES AND PROCEDURES

Subject: **PROPERTY DAMAGE** Section: ADMINISTRATION

PURPOSE: To curtail abuse and misuse of equipment and/or property, by charging repair expense to the responsible department. This will increase employee sensitivity to costs; and the net will result in reduced operating expense.

POLICY: The Chief Engineer is to implement, control and administrative the Property Damage Policy.

STANDARDS:
1. The policy applies to all damage caused by negligence and is not classified as **normal wear and tear**.
2. The Chief Engineer must determine whether or not the damage could have been prevented by proper training and/or supervision.
3. The Chief Engineer is to establish the cost for repair and/or replacement.
4. A Damage Report Form must be submitted to the General Manager for approval, and a copy sent to the head of the department responsible.
5. The Controller is to allocate cost to the responsible department.

PROCEDURES
1. The Chief Engineer is to assess the damage and determine if it is normal wear and tear or the result of employee abuse.
2. If it is determined that the damage was preventable, the Chief Engineer is to complete a Property Damage Report Form as in Figure 1.
3. The Property Damage Report Form is to be completed as follows:

   DAMAGED EQUIPMENT/PROPERTY - Description of damage.

   DATE DAMAGE REPORTED

   LOCATION OF DAMAGE - Area of hotel/property where damage occurred, i.e. laundry, kitchen, ballroom, etc.

   DESCRIPTION/DETAILS OF DAMAGE - Concise, accurate description of damage of item (s) or area (s).

PROPERTY OPERATIONS POLICIES AND PROCEDURES

Subject:	PROPERTY DAMAGE	Section: ADMINISTRATION
x		

ESTIMATE COST OF REPAIR/REPLACEMENT - Enter cost estimate, including material and labour. Enter estimated replacement cost if item needs to be **replaced**.

CAUSE OF DAMAGE - Indicate the cause of damage, if it can be determined; otherwise, describe probable cause. Also include comments such as: has similar damage occurred previously; was incident preventable; discussion with Department Head etc.

4. After completing the above, both the Department Head and the Chief Engineer are to sign the report and submit it to the General Manager for review and signature.

5. After repairs and/or replacement work is completed, the actual total cost (including material, labour and outside contractors) is to be entered on the report.

6. The Property Damage Report is then submitted to the Controller, for signature and allocation of expense to the responsible department.

7. In case the damage requires immediate attention, work should be completed and the Property Damage Report form completed at a later date.

8. The Chief Engineer must ensure that R&M is not charged with the associated costs, and if repairs are completed prior to the General Manager's approval, the costs are to be recovered to the R&M budget.

9. A copy of each Property Damage Report is to be maintained in department files.

Subject: **PROPERTY DAMAGE**	Section: ADMINISTRATION	Number: 1.6 Page: 3 of 3

Figure 1. - PROPERTY DAMAGE REPORT FORM

DAMAGED EQUIPMENT/PROPERTY: _____ DATE REPORTED: _____

LOCATION OF DAMAGED: _____

DESCRIPTION/DETAILS OF DAMAGE: _____
_____
_____
_____
_____

ESTIMATED COST OF REPAIR/REPLACEMENT:

Repair Cost _____ Replacement Cost _____

CAUSE OF DAMAGE/COMMENTS: _____
_____
_____

DEPARTMENT: _____

ACCOUNT NO. _____ ACTUAL COST _____

PROPERTY OPERATIONS POLICIES AND PROCEDURES

Subject:		Section: ADMINISTRATION
	WORK ORDER CONTRACT SUMMARY	

PURPOSE: To monitor costs associated with contracted labour which is expensed to Property Operations.

POLICY: The Chief Engineer is to implement the Work Order Contracts Summary Policy.

STANDARDS:
1. Work Order Contracts must be used for all contracted labour.
2. The Work Order Contract Summary report is to be completed monthly.
3. The Summary report is to be maintained on file.

PROCEDURES
1. Any work performed within the hotel by outside contractors which is expensed to Property Operations must be issued by a Hospitality Hotels & Resorts Corporate Work Order Contract. Purchase Orders are not to be used for outside labour.

2. The monthly Work Order Contract Summary is to be completed for each Hospitality Hotels & Resorts fiscal month, See Figure 1.

3. The Monthly Work Order Summary Form is completed as follows: Date of Issue - The date contract is issued.

   Contractor - Name of contractor/company.

   Cost - Includes all labour, materials, taxes and delivery costs associated with the contract.

   Reason - A brief description of the work, i.e. replace broken windows, roof repairs, condenser water pump rebuild, etc.

   Total Cost - Add total cost for the month for all work order contracts.

   Total Cost Year to Date - Add totals of each month year to date.

4. The monthly Summary is to be utilized as aid in monitoring your monthly R&M expenses, developing the annual R&M budget and analyzing Department staffing (i.e. skill level, number of employees).

Subject: **WORK ORDER CONTRACT SUMMARY**	Section ADMINISTRATION	Number: 1.7	Page 2 of 3

5. The Monthly Work Order Contract Summary is to be maintained in Department files.

6. If the department has a personal computer, or access to one, it is recommended that the Work Order Contract Summary be maintained on the computer.

PROPERTY OPERATIONS POLICIES AND PROCEDURES

Subject:	WORK ORDER CONTRACT SUMMARY	Section: ADMINISTRATION

PURPOSE: To monitor costs associated with contracted labour which is expensed to Property Operations.

POLICY: The Chief Engineer is to implement the Work Order Contracts Summary Policy.

STANDARDS:
1. Work Order Contracts must be used for all contracted labour.
2. The Work Order Contract Summary report is to be completed monthly.
3. The Summary report is to be maintained on file.

PROCEDURES
1. Any work performed within the hotel by outside contractors which is expensed Pe ratio ns must to Pro per ty be initiated by a hotel purchase order.
2. The monthly Work Order Contract Summary is to be completed for each Hospitality Hotel s & Resorts fiscal month. See Figure 1.
3. The Monthly Work Order Summary Form is completed as follows:
   Date of Issue - The date contract is issued

   Contractor - Name of contractor/company.

   Cost - Includes all labour, materials, taxes and delivery costs associated with the contract.

   Reason - A brief description of the work, i.e. replace broken windows, roof repairs, condenser water pump rebuild, etc.
   Total Cost - Add total cost for the month for all work order contracts. Total Cost

   Year to Date - Add totals of each month year to date.

4. The monthly Summary is to be utilized as an aid in monitoring your monthly R&M expenses, developing the annual O&M budget and analyzing Department staffing (i.e. skill level, number of employees).

| Subject: **WORK ORDER CONTRACT SUMMARY** | Section ADMINISTRATION | Number: 1.7 | Page 2 of 3 |

5. The monthly Work Order Contract Summary is to be maintained in Department files.

6. If the department has a personal computer, or access to one, it is recommended that the Work Order Contract Summary be maintained on the computer.

Subject:	Section	Number: 1.7	Page 3 of 3
WORK ORDER CONTRACT SUMMARY	ADMINISTRATION		

FIGURE 1 - MONTHLY WORK ORDER CONTRACT SUMMARY FROM EXAMPLE

WORK ORDER CONTRACT SUMMARY

For the Month of: ,19

Dte Issue	Con tractor	Cost	Reason
		Total Cost:	
		Total cost year to date:	

_____
Chief Engineer

PROPERTY OPERATIONS POLICIES AND PROCEDURES

Subject:	MONTHLY REPORT	Section: ADMINISTRATION

PURPOSE: To provide a system for reporting the current status of the Engineering Department to the Divisional/Regional Director of Engineering and the hotel General Manager.

POLICY: The Chief Engineer will implement the **MONTHLY REPORT** policy.

STANDARDS:
1. The Monthly Report form will be used.
2. The Monthly Report will be completed each month.
3. The Monthly Report will be submitted to the Divisional/Regional Director of Engineering and Hotel General Manager no later than three (3) days following Fiscal closing.

PROCEDURE: The **MONTHLY REPORT** will consist of the following:

1. **MONTHLY** LETTER scheduled in to the following sections (sample as per Figure 1):

    c. **RED FLAG ITEMS**

      Identify any serious department problems, delays, hazards or incidents. If there is nothing to report, write **NONE**.

    g. **Hospitality**
       IT
       List number of guest rooms completed versus monthly quota. If unable to complete quota, state reasons.

    k. **REPAIR LOG**

      Indicate current status of the repair log. If not current, give reasons and state when repair log will be up to date.

    o. **PREVENTIVE MAINTENANCE**

      Give the status of the schedule established for the month. If unable to complete work scheduled, explain ed and indicate when work will be up to date.

Subject:	Section	Number: 1.8	Page 2 of 19
MONTHLY REPORT	ADMINISTRATION		

a. **FIRE PROTECTION PREVENTIVE MAINTENANCE**

Give the status of the schedule established for the month. If unable to complete work scheduled, explain and indicate when work will be up to date.

e. **WORK REQUEST**

Report number of request issued, completed and backlogs.

i. **SAFETY TAGS/LOCKOUT**

Report on the use and effectiveness of this accident prevenation Policy.

m. **IN-HOUSE PROJECTS**

Describe briefly any major in house projects involving the Engineering Department and indicate estimated completion dates.

q. **CAPITAL PROJECTS**

Describe briefly capital projects in progress and indicate estimated completion dates.

2. **LIFE AND FIRE SAFETY PROTECTION COMPLIANCE SCHEDULE**

A list of legend number and a list of description are attached to this Policy. It is important that each description be read as you fill the compliance date sheet, as the information reflects the most recent Hospitality Hotels & Resorts Policy regarding Life and Fire Safety.

Upon receipt of the report (each month) the information will be reviewed including the projected date of compliance for those items not in compliance.

A six months report depicting the percentage of compliance of all hotels will be generated and sent to all Chief Engineers and General Managers for information.

Subject: **MONTHLY REPORT**	Section ADMINISTRATION	Number: 1.8	Page 3 of 19

FIGURE 1. - **MONTHLY LETTER EXAMPLE**

    TO : REGIONAL DIRECTOR OF ENGINEERING   DATE:

    FROM: DOE/CE   COPY: GENERAL MANAGER

    SUBJECT: MONTHLY REPORT FOR (month)

IX. RED FLAG ITEMS

    Trash compactor controls not in compliance with OSHA and Hospitality Hotels & Resorts Standards. Contractor advised to immediately install constant-pressure push button and access door interlock.

XIII. POLICY/PROCEDURE STATUS

    Hospitality-It - Quota for the month is 166 rooms. Due to vacation schedule, only 150 were completed. Will complete full quota this month.

    Repair Log -Allentir spostedandlogup-t-odateA.ge and repair history on kitchen exhaust fan indicates replacement necessary.

    Preventive Maintenance -All worksheet for the month were completed.

    Fire Protection Preventive Maintenance - All weekly schedule sheets for the month completed.

    Work Request - Policy functioning property except for minor problem with duplicated work requests. Will review procedure at next Department Head Meeting.

    Safety Tag/Lockout - Program being strictly enforced. Department members understand the importance of the system and use tags and lock-outs.

XXVII. PROJECT STATUS

    inhouse Projects - Installing floor to ceiling bookshelves in accounting office. To be completed by March 15.

    Capital Projects - Project No. 88-4 (Security safes in guest rooms closets) 60 percent complete. Full completion expected by April 1".

Compliance Schedule Legend Numbers

1. Floor and wall penetrations sealed
2. Fire dampers started in ductworks
3. Duct doors fire rated
4. Floor slabs in duct shafts
5. Guest room doors fire rated
6. Escape/Exit doors fire rated
7. Guest room door closer for compartmentation
8. Shaft walls fire rated enclosures
9. Emergency exits to street level
10. Atrium smoke exhausting system
11. Atrium understairs floors with smoke detectors
12. Areas separated by fire doors walls and floors
13. Hazardous areas separated by rated enclosures
14. Smoke detectors installed throughout
15. Heat detectors in kitchens
16. Manual alarm stations in public areas and B O TH
17. Centralized fire alarm control stations
18. Fire control panels attended continuously
19. Detection and protection systems on emergency power
20. Fire alarm annunciation in all areas
21. Guest on same floor alerted of fire
22. Building-wide evacuation for building < 3 stories high
23. Emergency broadcasting to all occup B1'f19
24. Elevators return to street level up alarm
25. Fire alarm to fire department automatically
26. Dead end controllers less than six meters
27. Fire escape exit signs provided
28. Fire exit sign sized of illumination
29. Escape signs lighted and on emergency power
30. Minimum of 2 exits per floor
31. Fire sprinklers provided to all areas
32. Sprinklers to Sheraton fire safety standards
33. Minimum residual pressure for sprinklers
34. Automatic kitchen hood extinguisher
35. Transformer and electrical rooms protected
36. **Hose Reel Inn all areas**
37. Standpipes in all emergency stairways
38. Portable extinguishers provided all areas
39. Portable extinguishers location
40. All areas with n 30 meters of fire hose
41. Water supply at 2270 L/min (500 GPM) for 30 minutes minimum
42. Water pressure at minimum of 448 KPA (65 PSI)
43. Grade a water supply
44. Secondary water storage minimum 30 minutes
45. Fireman elevator available
46. Fire extinguishing system signals to alarm panel
47. Interior finish materials certified
48. Conformance to local codes
49. Fire prevention PM program Implemented Employee
50. fire brigade training program Implemented

35

Subject:	Section	Number: 1.8	Page 5 of 19
MONTHLY REPORT	ADMINISTRATION		

Life & Fire Safety Protection
Compliance Schedule

Legend Number	Description
	Compartmentation
1.	Are all penetrations formed by conduits, piping and ductwork passing through fire rated floors and walls sealed off with fire rated sealant? To the full thickness of the wall?
2.	Are fire dampers provided in heating, ventilation and air conditioning ducts, which pass through fire barrier wall of 2 hour fire rating and above?
3.	Are all pipe and service duct doors fire rated to 1 hour?
4.	Are floor slabs constructed in all the pipe duct and service shafts?
5.	Are all guest room doors fire rated to 1 hour?
6.	
7.	Are all escape door/emergency exit doors fire rated to 1 ½ hours?
8.	Are all guest room doors provided with automatic self-closing devices for compartmentation purposes?
	Are all shaft in the hotel protected by 2-hour fire rated enclosures?
	iii. Ventilation shafts
	iv. Electrical wiring shafts
	v. Mechanical equipment shafts
	vi. Rubbish shafts
	vii. Linen chutes
	viii. Dumb waiters
	ix. Elevator shafts
9.	Do all emergency exits open directly to street level?
	If an atrium of more than 2 floors exists is the following true:
10.	i. Smoke exhaust system provided?
11.	Smoke detectors are provided for each underside floor protruding into the atrium?
12.	Are all the areas of different uses separated by fire resistive doors, walls and floors?(Areas of different uses are: residential, restaurants, storage, office, kitchens, plant rooms).

Subject:	Section	Number: 1.8
MONTHLY REPORT	ADMINISTRATION	

13. Are all hazardous areas separated from other parts of the building by fire resisting barriers of 2 or 3 hours?
14. Are smoke detectors provided in all following areas?
    - iii. Guest rooms and corridors
    - iv. Public areas
    - v. Offices
    - vi. Assembly areas (function rooms)
    - vii. Back of the house areas Mechanical
    - viii. and electrical rooms
    - ix. Restaurants
    - x. Storage areas
15. Are heat detectors provided in all kitchens?
16. Are manual alarm stations provided in public areas and BOTH as per Hospitality Hotels & Resorts Fire Safety Guidelines?
17. Is there a central control station to monitor the fire detection and fire protection system?
18. Is the central fire control panel located in a room which is constantly attended by trained personnel?
19. Are the fire detection and fire protection systems on the emergency power supply?
20. Is fire alarm annunciation provided in all areas as per Hospitality Hotel & Resorts Fire Safety Standards?
21. Are all guests on the same floor of the alarm, as well as the floor above and below, alerted when a fire alarm is activated?
22. For buildings less than three (3) stories in height only, will the actuation of the fire alarm automatically sound the building wide evacuation alarm ?
23. I s an em ergenc y broadcasting system available for communication with all the occupants of the building?
24. Will all the elevators in the building return to street level when a fire alarm is activated?
25. Will the fire alarm signals be automatically transmitted to the local fire department?

Escape Routes and Emergency Power

26. Is the maximum travel distance in any dead end corridor less than Gm?
27. Are all Exit signs prom in entity displayed?
28. Are all fire exit signs of the correct size and illumination characteristics as per Hospitality Hotels & Resorts Fire Safety Standards?
29. Are all escape signs illuminated and also on the emergency power supply system?
30. Are there at least two independent fire exits provided on every floor?

37

Subject: **MONTHLY REPORT**	Section ADMINISTRATION	Number: 1.8	Page 7 of 19

Fire Extinguishing System

31. Is an automatic sprinkler system provided for all the following areas?

    iii. Guest rooms and corridors
    iv. Public areas
    v. Offices
    vi. Assembly areas (function room)
    vii. Back of the house areas
    viii. Mechanical and electrical rooms
    ix. Restaurants
    x. Storage areas
    xi. Kitchen 1s

32. Does the design for the automatic sprinkler system meet with Hospitality Hotels & Resorts Fire Safety Standards?

33. Is the minimum residual pressure of at least 103 kpa (15psi) available at the highest sprinklers?

34. Is an automatic extinguishing system provided for all kitchen hoods?

35. Are the transformer and electrical switchboard rooms protected with any of the following systems:

    iii. Halon
    iv. Portable extinguishers
    v. Smoke Detectors CO_2
    vi. Dry Chemical
    vii. Sprinklers
    viii.

36. Are 1 inch hose reels provided in the building in all the following areas as per Hospitality Hotels & Resorts Fire Safety Standards?

    iii. Guest room corridor
    iv. Public areas
    v. Back of the house

37. Are standpipe systems provided in all emergency staircase as per Hospitality Hotels & Resort Fire Safety Standards?

38. Are portable fire extinguishers of the correct type provided in all areas?

39. Are all portable fire extinguishers located in a permanent position, free of obstructions, clearly visible and within easy reach?

40. Are all areas in the building within 30 meters reach of a 25mm or 40mm fire hose?

41. Is the water supply for the standpipe system sufficient to provide at least 1.89 cu.m/min (500GPM) for at least 30 minutes?

42. Is the minimum water supply pressure at the most remote standpipe hose connection more than 448 kpa (65 psi)?

43. Is the water supply for the fire protection system a dual feed supply? (from two separate sources)

Subject:	Section	Number: 1.8	Page 8 of 19
MONTHLY REPORT	ADMINISTRATION		

44. In case storage tanks supplement the street mains as a secondary water source for fire protection, is the duration of the secondary water supply at least 30 minutes?

45. Is there an elevator available for the dedicated use by the local fire brigade for fire fighting purposes?

46. Is the operation of any part of the extinguishing system, i.e.: fire pumps, flow switches, tamper switches, hose reels, kitchen extinguishing systems, etc. automatically signaled to the central fire alarm control panel?

47. Have materials used for: interior finishes, carpets, furniture cushions, draperies, upholstery fabrics, bed covers, bed mattresses, wallcoverings, been tested for flame retardation and toxic fume generation? Are fire rating certificates available ?

48. Are all buildings of the property constructed in compliance with local building codes relating to fire resistive construction by building class, size and occupancy?

49. Is the Hospitality Hotels & Resorts Fire Prevention Preventive Maintenance Program in effect as per Sheraton's Safety - Security Loss Control Manual, Section **4.11**a?

50. Is the Hospitality Hotels & Resorts Employee **Fire Brigade Training** Program in effect?

| Subject: **MONTHLY REPORT** | Section ADMINISTRATION | Number: 1.8 | Page 9 of 19 |

Life & Fire Safety Protection
Compliance Schedule

For the Month of: __199___

Line Number	Copy1 Yes/No	Life in Compliance what is the current Status?	Projected Date of Compliance
1			
2			
3			
4			
5			
6			
7			
8			
9			
10			
11			
12			
13			
14			
15			
16			
17			
18			
19			
20			
21			
22			
23			
24			
25			
26			

Subject: MONTHLY REPORT	Section ADMINISTRATION	Number: 1.8

Legend Number	Comply Yes/No	If item is not in Compliance what is the current Status?	Projected Date of Compliance
27			
28			
29			
30			
31			
32			
33			
34			
35			
36			
37			
38			
39			
40			
41			
42			
43			
44			
45			
46			
47			
48			
49			
50			

Chief Engineer	
Date	

Subject:	Section	Number: 1.8	Page 11 of 19
MONTHLY REPORT	ADMINISTRATION		

Environmental Health, Safety & Security Committee Meetings

The Environmental Health, Safety & Security Committee should be held **once a month** a meeting, preferably at the same time and place each month. The meeting should last no longer than one hour. The chairman prepares an agenda and distribute it in advance to assure a well-organized, productive meeting. The General Manager is urged to attend as many meeting as possible.

The purpose of this meeting is to review the preceding month's accidents, to identify hazards and document them, to develop corrective action, and to follow up until the hazards are controlled or eliminated. It is essential that the minutes represents a complete record of all items and recommendations emerging from the discussions in order to assure effective, comprehensive and corrective actions. This detailed record does not only provide a vehicle to follow up on recommendation but also becomes a **legal record** of preventive measures taken in the interest of guest, employees and Fire Safety.

Instructions for completing the minutes are on the following pages. In order to maximize the Committee's productivity, it is recommended that the Chairman follows carefully this outline and related instructions. While doing so the efficiency will be maximized and repetition of previous discussions or deviation from relevant issues will be avoided.

An example of a hotel Environmental Health, Safety & Security Committee Meeting minutes in accordance with the form is located in the Safety & Security Loss Control Manual, Section 4. **Each hotel** should build up their reports according to this example.

As an ongoing follow-up procedure, each member of the Committee should communicate with superiors and employees about the pertinent items discussed within the meeting.

Subject:	Section	Number: 1.8	Page 12 of 19
MONTHLY REPORT	ADMINISTRATION		

Instructions for Preparing Minutes of the Environmental Health Safety & Security Committee Meeting

Name of Hotel   Deatfismeeting:
Date of last meeting.   Member exo tin:

Name   Position 11
(Names and positions of permanent members attending.)

Members Absent Position:

Name   Position
(Names and position of permanent members not attending, reason for absence and substitutes' 11 ame and position.)

Introduction of guests a11 invited employees.

(Names and position of employees invited 10 participate this month and names of outside guests).

Review of Accidents, Security Incidents and Inspection Checklists

• Review of Accidents

This is a monthly analysis of all guest a11d employee accidents that were reported on the Accident Summary sheets a11d Accident Investigation forms as well as near misses that were observed or brought to a member's attention. All causes should be discussed in order to undertake the appropriate action 11. Numbers of lost work 11g days per accide11l should also be recorded.

In order to have an effective discussion about employee accidents, the following should be kept in mind when receiving the Accide11ts Investigation form:

- Where did the accident happen?
- How did the accident happen?
- What unsafe co11 edition s and unsafe acts were involved?
- Was the employee properly trained for the job?
- Was the employee doing what he/she was supposed to do at the time of the accident?
- Where was the supervisor and other employees during the acclde11t?
- Was the injured person in good health on the day of the accide11t?
- What temporary measures should be take11 to prevent reoccurrence?
- What should be done to prevent on a permanent basis similar accidents?
- Was immediate notice given to the insura11ce compa11y?

B. Security Incidents (To be listed on a separate page)

All security incidents should be reviewed for common sense solutions a11d preventive measures.

43

Subject:	Section	Number: 1.8	Page 13 of 19
MONTHLY REPORT	ADMINISTRATION		

C. Inspection Items Requiring Discussion

Planned inspections are required to detect in a systematic and timely manner. The inspector should be the supervisor who knows his/her area of responsibility and what conditions to look for. However, it is recommended that assignments be rotated at least every six months for the benefit of a fresh perspective because a department can become too familiar to a supervisor and a hazard may be overlooked.

As hazards are discovered, immediate steps should be taken to correct them. The solution should get at the root of the problem not just be a superficial remedy. It is the Committee's response ib il ty to monitor inspections , discuss those in sp ec tion items requiring committee action, and assure that necessary corrections are made.

In the Safety & Security Loss Control Manual you will find :

5.A master checklist for general hazards
6.A master checklist for fire prevention
7.Specific individual departmental checklists to be used as a supplement to the master sheets.

This checklists are provided as a guide from which each hotel is expected to develop its own checklist. While the checklist was developed based on the most commonly found deficiencies in hotels, they are not inclusive.

No hotel should assume that by using the checklist as they will have met all mandatory occupational safety and health requirements of their country, state, city or region. It is the responsibility of each hotel to develop its own checklists based on the standards appropriate for its geographic location and the characteristics of the hotel. Please Note that space has been left at the end of each checklist for use for hotels in adding their own questions.

Items Completed Since Last Meetings

This includes all items completed in a satisfactory manner since the last meeting. If the steps taken are not permanent solutions, the items should then be included in the "-Pi sending Item s" section .

Pending Items

This is a review of those hazards or problems identified but not yet controlled or solved due to time problems, complexity of steps involved, or other delays. Items will remain in this category until completed and reported in the above section. Adequate reasons are to be given for each delay.

If the committee finds that an identified hazard cannot be corrected within ninety (90) days, alternate recommendations, (such as training) are to be developed.

Miscellaneous

This is a discussion of items not mentioned above such as review of new governmental requirements, outside speakers, establishment of first aid classes. safety campaigns/programs, review of new training materials, update and/or review of Hospitality Hotels & Resorts Safety and Security procedures, etc. Whenever these discussions results in a decision and an action item, these items are to be listed under the "New Items" section

Subject:	Section	Number: 1.8	Page 14 of 19
MONTHLY REPORT	ADMINISTRATION		

New Items

This is a statement of all new items stemming from the discussions held for the above sections or mentioned at this time. All items should be recorded for appropriate follow-up. Assignments and due dates for completion and should be included.

Review of Loss Control Manual or Other Environmental Health, Safety/ Security-Related Material

The Chairman will review any pertinent safety/security material received from headquarters or elsewhere with the group. Review of the Loss Control Manual will be conducted as needed. The invited employees will be encouraged to review the manual at their convenience.

Each member of the Committee should be provided with a 3 ring (or similar) **binder** to be called the Environmental Health, Safety & Security Committee Notebook. The Committee members are to lace the meeting form, All Committee Meeting Minutes, and other safety materials in the binder for future reference or transfer to members, Committee members are to bring this binder to each meeting.

Attachments:

All items referred to as attachments in this section are located in the Hospitality Hotels & Resorts Safety & Security Loss Control Manual Section 4. The distribution of Minutes of Meetings shall be in accordance with Corporate/Divisional requirements.

Note: The above form must be followed. Use as many pages as necessary to provide the above information.

| Subject: **MONTHLY REPORT** | Section ADMINISTRATION | Number: 1.8 | Page 15 of 19 |

<u>Instructions for Filling Out Monthly Accident and Incident Report (M.A.I.R)</u>
This report indicates the actual number and classification of occupational related injuries, illnesses or incidents which have occurred during the calendar month. Enter the totals as follows:

Classification	Definition
First Aid	Treatment administered by a person of some knowledge about First aid, Registered Nurse or Medical Doctor in which treatment is limited to:

- Application of Antiseptics on first visit to a doctor or nurse.
- Bandaging on any visit to a doctor or nurse.
- Treatment of burns of first degree
- Compresses, hot or cold, on first visit to a doctor or nurse only.
- Use of elastic bandage on first visit to a doctor or nurse only.
- Removal of foreign bodies not imbedded, or irrigation of eye.
- Removal of foreign bodies from wound by tweezers or other simple techniques.
- Use of non prescription medications.
- Observation of injury on second or subsequent visit
- Use of ointments applied to abrasion to prevent drying or cracking.
- Tetanus shots, initial or boosters alone
- Hospitalization for observation (no other **treatment** than **first** aid).
- x-ray which is negative.

B. Medical Without Lost Workdays (Excluding Date of Injury)

Injuries requiring more advance treatment by a registered nurse or medical doctor. Advance treatment includes:

- Antiseptics applied on second or subsequent visit to a doctor or nurse.
- Treatment of burns of second or third degree
- Butterfly sutures (stitches)
- compresses, hot or cold, on second or subsequent visit to a doctor or nurse.
- cutting away dead skin (surgical debridement)
- Diathermy treatment.
- Removal of foreign bodies if embedded in eye.
- Removal of foreign bodies from wound by a physician because of depth of embedment, size or shape of object(s).
- Treatment for infection
- Prescription medications used
- Soaking, hot or cold, on second or subsequent visit
- Sutures (stitches)
- Whirlpool treatment
- x-ray which is positive.

C. Total Lost Workdays Cases This Month

occupational illness or injury other than a fatality which results in lost workdays, not including the date of injury.

Subject:	Section	Number: 1.8	Page 16 of 19
MONTHLY REPORT	ADMINISTRATION		

D1. Total Lost Workdays a/b	The number of occupational injury or illness related work days lost this month.
	a = Days lost from this month's cases (excluding date of injury)
	b = Days lost from accidents which occurred in previous month (s)
D2. c/d	The number of occupational injury or illness related work days lost year-to-date.
	c = Days lost from this year's cases (excluding date of injury)
	d = Days still lost from accidents which occurred in previous year (s).
E. Fatality	Occupational injury or illness resulting in death. (Notify TSC Safety Department within 8 days).
F. Fire	Fire losses of any amount. (Forward written report to TSC Safety Department within 24 hours. **Major Fires Notify TSC Safety Department IMMEDIATELY.**
G. Other	Accidental incidents involving physical losses to building and equipment, or business interruption due to windstorm, flood, riot, loss of utilities, etc.
H. Number of Employees	Total number of employees covered by this report
I. Injuries/ or Fatalities	Public Liability accidents, including food claims and fatalities. (All fatalities must be reported to TSC Safety Department within 8 hours).
J. Property Loss Incidents	Any guest losses due to theft, damage or misplacement of property.

The Monthly Accident and Incident Report must be attached to the General Manager's Monthly Letter and the Safety Committee Minutes.

These must be forwarded to **TSC Safety Department** within **7 days** after the end of the month being reported on.

Hospitality Hotels & Resorts management practices, Hospitality Hotels & Resorts has established three critical goals:

- **Improve Fire and Life Safety**
- **Reduce the Amount of Pollution We Generate**
- **Correct Identified Environment and Safety Problems Promptly**

In order for Hospitality Hotels & Resorts to measure progress in these areas. Hospitality Hotels & Resorts has established four statistical measures of which three apply to Hospitality Hotels & Resorts as further described in the attached.

We have combined the former Hospitality Hotels & Resorts (MAIR) Monthly Accident and Incident Report and the statistics now required monthly by Hospitality Hotel & Resort into the **Monthly Environment & Safety Metrics Report.** So far, reporting compliance has been satisfactory.

However, questions generated from the hotels indicate that further explanation of some of the measurement categories is required:

Question: Why change the former monthly Accident Frequency Index Formula from $\frac{1B + CI \times 100 \times 12}{H \times N}$ to $\frac{1B + CI \times 100}{H}$?

Answer: The former formula resulted in an index that showed the year's average accident index if the accident trend as established in the (calculated) month would continue. The Hospitality Hotel & Resort-required formula shows the actual percentage of accidents during the reported month. (This is not a typographical error as some thought). Please note the requirement to calculate and report year-to-date Accident Frequency index still continues.

Division Engineers
Director of Technical Services
August 2007
Page 2

Question 2: What constitute "Cost of Managing Waste"?

Answer: The Cost of Management Waste includes all waste from food and hotel operations, including hazardous waste, ordinary solid waste, on-site waste treatment, and waste removal, and disposal of off-site waste treatment cost. The cost of all waste handling associated with hotel labor should be included.

Although ideally all hotels would use exactly the same waste cost handling criteria, it is more important that the hotels are consistent in using (month to month) the same cost measurement criteria so each hotel can measure its own progress in waste (cost) reduction.

Question 3: Why are we (Hospitality Hotels & Resorts) interested in obtaining these new statistic?

Answer: Primarily, by identifying total waste management costs, we can establish incentives and goals to reduce, through the appropriate purchase of materials, recycling, and efficient work practices, our negative impact on the environment.

Further adjustment of the statistical reporting frequency and formulas may need to be done to make the numbers as meaningful as possible. In the meantime, however, please provide the hotel with your assistance to ensure efforts are being made to meet the three goals and make the reported numbers as credible as possible.

Best regards,

Note: The Monthly Environment & Safety Metrics Report replaces the former Monthly and Quarterly Accident and Incident Report. We Have a reporting obligation to Hospitality Hotels & Resorts, so please encourage the hotels to send their reports to us promptly.

Environment and Safety Metrics

Implementation Guide

Introduction

We have begun integrating Environment and Safety (ES) concerns (environmental protection, industrial hygiene, safety, and fire using statistical measures (metrics), we will track progress in meeting three critical ES program goals:

6. Improving safety.
7. Reducing the amount of pollution we generate.
8. Correcting identified ES problem promptly.

Two of the metrics identified are currently being computed on a regular basis; the data used to compute the remaining metrics are already being collected by most Hospitality Hotels & Resorts Units. The guide explains the metrics, and their computation and presentation format; and the process of setting targets (goals) for them. Also included is a schedule for implementing the ES metrics.

Responsibilities and Reporting

Implementation of this integration effort and the reporting of progress in achieving ES goals is an operating management responsibility. Initially, company presidents are to submit to their respective senior Hospitality Hotels & Resorts HQ executives the proposed metrics adapted for their operations, describing the specific wastes and chemicals their units will track. After approval by Hospitality Hotels & Resorts HQ, company presidents are to submit proposed goals for 2008 for each of their metrics.

Companies must include descriptions of the approved metrics and the goals for 2008 in the next Operating Plan, using agreed upon reporting formats. Monthly progress reports are to be submitted upon full implementation of metrics in 2008 When performance is below the target, backup charts and information must be used to explain gaps, and the actions to be taken, or the resources needed, to close them.

Environment and Safety personnel at all levels will provide technical assistance and support to assure timely implementation and full communication of management decisions regarding the integration of ES concerns into management functions.

ES Metrics

The five initial metrics Hospitality Hotels & Resorts will address are 1) injury severity, 2) injury frequency, 3) cost of managing process waste, 4) volume of materials of concern purchased, and 5) consolidated action plan delinquency. Four of the five are required for all Hospitality Hotels & Resorts operating companies. The "volume of materials of concern purchased" is only required for manufacturing companies.

Companies are to follow the instructions provided in this guide to calculate each of the metrics, and, where indicated, chose as appropriate factor for their operations.

Beginning in April, companies are to collect the needed data, calculate the metrics, and promptly report to Hospitality Hotels & Resorts Headquarters the result of the initial calculations, along with any suggested improvements.

Setting Goals

The trial period will provide the bases for improvement targets (goals) for each of the metrics. ES goals will be set after the appropriate metrics have been determined for each of the companies. Goals will be a challenge for each company to achieve, and will require effort consistent with other business goals.

Environment and safety personnel will give full support to line managers in identifying cost-effective alternatives to achieve ES goals. Application of the Hospitality Hotels & Resorts Process Safety and Pollution Prevention analytical process should be considered in this effort.

Implementation Schedule

The following are the steps the companies and Hospitality Hotels & Resorts HQ will take this year to implement ES metrics and further the integration of ES concerns into business management:

·Companies develop the bases for the materials of concern and begin gathering ES data. (April)

·Companies report initial data for the April period and propose improvements in the metrics to Hospitality Hotels & Resorts Headquarters. (May)

·Hospitality Hotels & Resorts Headquarters reviews companies' IS data and makes appropriate changes in the metrics, as required. (May-June)

·Hospitality Hotels & Resorts HQ establishing ES goals for 2008 (August)

·Companies incorporate metrics into 2007-08 Operating Plans. (September-November)

Metric: Injury Severity (IS)

Description: This measure tracks the severity of injuries suffered in lost-time accidents, as an indication of the impact accidents are having upon productivity and cost of labor.

Application: The measure is required for all operating companies. Data should be recorded at each site and consolidated for the company report.

Computation: Either use the Hospitality Hotels & Resorts Injury and Illness, and Lost Workday Indices (See Hospitality Hotels & Resorts HE'S Management Practices 20.4), or compute directly.

$$IS = \frac{\text{Hospitality Hotels \& Resorts Lost Workday Index}}{\text{Hospitality Hotels \& Resorts Injury and Illness Index}} = \frac{D}{B+C}$$

D = days of work lost
C = number of lost-workday cases

If computed directly, the values must be adjusted each month to assign any lost workdays in the current month to lost workdays cases from any prior month.

Computation frequency: Monthly, calculate new values and update the 12-month running average.

Construct a graph with the following information:
    the monthly values
    the 12-month running average
    the 12-month running average for 1993
    the goal for 1994
A sample chart is included.

Reporting frequency: Provide in a separate monthly report and include in every Operations Review.

Metric : Injury Frequency (IF)

Description: This measure tracks the number of accidents resulting in lost-time or medical treatment that occur per 100 employees. It is similar to the Hospitality Hotels & Resorts Injury Index now in use.

Application: This measure is required for all operating companies and should be recorded at each site.

Computation:

$$IF = \frac{(B + C) \times 100}{H}$$

B = number of medical cases in the reporting period.
C = number of lost-workday cases in the reporting period
H = average number of employees in reporting period

Compute the 12-month running average using the same formula.

Computation frequency: Monthly, calculate new values and update the 12-month running average.

Construct a graph with the following information:
- the monthly values
- the 12-month running average
- the 12-month running average for 1993
- the goal for 1994

A sample chart is included.

Reporting frequency: Provide in a separate monthly report and include in every operations Review.

Metric: Cost of Managing Process Waste (CW)

Description: This measures tracks the cost of handling waste. The choice of this measure is based on the assumption that lowering these costs will result in the reduction in usage of the materials disposed or more effective use of them in internal processes. "Handling" is meant to include on-site waste treatment and material transfer costs, including the associated labor, as well as payment for off-site disposal or treatment.

"Process waste" is meant to include all waste, hazardous waste, ordinary solid waste, or a combination of the last two. Each company must define the specific components of its metric, subject to Hospitality Hotels & Resorts HQ approval.

Application: This measure is required for all operating companies and should be recorded at each site.

Computation:

$$CW = \frac{W}{P}$$

W = cost of handling waste (U.S> Dollars)

P = number of units produced or sales (U.S. Dollars) in reporting period, chosen so that the computed value of CW will be greater than unity

Computation frequency: Monthly, calculate new values and update the three-month running average.

Construct a graph with the following information:
· The monthly values
• A three-month running average
· The three-month running average for December 1993
· The goal for 1994
A sample chart is included

Reporting frequency: Provide In a separate monthly report and include in every Operations Review.

LEGEND

A	Employee First Aid Cases	One time treatment and subsequent observation of minor scratches, cuts, burns, splinters, etc. provided by a physician or registered professional person iie
B	Employee Medical Cases Without Lost Workdays	Treatment (other first aid) administered by a physician or by a registered professional under the standing orders of a physician II.
C	Employee Lost Workday Cases	Any occupational injuries or illness (other than fatalities) that result in lost workdays. Notify corporate. Fire, Safety & Environmental Health Department immediately if an employee fatality occurs. (Written report due within 72 hours).
D (a/band c/d)	Total employee Lost Workdays	The number of workdays, excluding the date of injury or onset of Baldness, that employees would have worked but could not because of occupation al injury or ilh1ess. b. Days lost from cases which occurred this mo1lth (excluding date of injury or onset of illness). c. Days lost this month from cases which occurred in previous month (s). d. Days lost (YTD) from cases which occurred this calendar year, Days lost (YTD) from cases which occurred in previous year (s).
E	Regulatory Citations	Formal 11otice of deficiency or non-compliance by federal, state, or local governing agency (OSHA. EPA, etc.)
F	Fires	Fire losses of any amount. Notify Fire. Life Safety & Env. Health Department within 24 hours. Report major fires immediately.
G	Chemical Spills	Accidental releases of corrosive or hazardous products.
H	Average Number of Full-time employees	This figure represents the average number of full-time equivalent employees, based on 40 hours per week. Year-to-date. (This number should be an average of the monthly figures reported on the hotel's FRS Monthly Input form).
I	Insurance Reportable Guest Injuries, Illnesses, or Fatalities	Public liabBy incidents. (Notify Corporate Fire, Life Safety and E1wironme11tal Health Department immediately of a guest fatality. (writte11 report due within 72 hours.)
N	Number of Months Reported	
p	Gross Sales	Gross sales in 100K units (U.S. Dollars)
T	Action Items Completed On Time	Number of corrective action 11 items identified through Health, E1w Iro11me111 & Safety Audits. Inspec tio11s by division staff. insurance company or other external consultant and completed on time within the reporting period.
U	Delinquent Action Items	Number of corrective action 11 items (as described above) that should have been, but were not, completed within 1 the reporting period.
W	Cost of Ha11ding Waste	All treatme11t a11d ordi11ary solid waste and hazardous disposal costs. including labor.

FORWARD ONE COPY OF THIS REPORT BY THE 10ᵗʰ DAY OF THE MONTH FOLLOWING THE MONTH BEING REPORTED TO:
Hospitality Hotels & Resorts

Subject:	Section	Number: 1.8	Page 18 of 19
MONTHLY REPORT	ADMINISTRATION		

Date: .

Cc: tyLer t r Safety Security
Committee
Corporate Safety-Security Dept

MONTHLY ACCIDENT AND INCIDENT REPORT

Hotel/Location/Property:

Month When Accidents/Incidents Occurred:

Category		Classification	This Month	Year to Date	Same MO. Last Year	Year to Date Last Year
	A	First Aid				
Employee Injuries and Illnesses	B	Medical Without Lost Workdays				
	C	Total Lost Workday Cases This M01ilh	1 2	3 4		
	D	Total Lost Wort<days This Month	a b	c d		
	E	Fatality				
Incidents	F	Fire				
	G	Others				
Staffing	H	Number of employees (Full Time Equivalent)				
Guest Accidents/incidents	I	Injuries and for Fatalities				
	J	Property Loss incide 11ts				
Governmental	K	Regulatory Citations Received				
employee Injury Index						

Safety Meeting Held   Date   _ Monthly Fire & Emergency Drill Held   Ti e/Dat   _
No of. Safety Recommendations Outstanding since last report
No of. Safety Recommendations Completed since last report

*See Reverse for explanations 11n d definitions.
"Oe1 1d litic for sub mitting this reper l together withS1 l fcty - Security Committee Meeting M nutes,is the 15 of the month to law 119 the mufiln being reported

Others:

PART2

PROGRAMS

2.0 PROGRAMS

2.1	Hospitality
2.2	Repair Log
2.3	Preventive Maintenance
2.4	Fire Protection Preventive Maintenance]
2.6	Safety Tag/Lockout
2.7	Thermographic survey

HOSPITALITY PROGRAM

PROGRAM

Saleable rooms are our most important source of profit, a whopping 70% of room revenue is profit! To protect this source of income the Program has been made mandatory in every resorts property.

Bosspitality _ who only fixes faucets, locks and numerous other little things is actually a very important person. All the little things that Bosspitality _ does is like polishing the proverbial apple and thereby keeps our product saleable. Without the guest room revenue, all the things we are doing don't need doing.

The Hospitality _ Program provides a fixed schedule and routine for maintaining function rooms and 25% of the guest room each month, while at the same time increases employee production. Production is increased by reducing "go for" time as tools and materials required are in the Hospitality _ cart.

The Hospitality _ cart should have the following characteristics: large wheels to roll easily over carpets, in and out of elevators, over door sills and brief steps, etc. Ample storage space, especially drawers and bins should be provided. Provisions must be made to lock the cart against theft.

The portable workshop may be ordered through the Hospitality Hotels & Resorts Supply Company. The unit is manufactured by the Roll-On Manufacturing Corp. and has a quality and character to complement the prestige of Hospitality Hotels & Resort. See Figure 1.

Guest room preventive maintenance is scheduled on a room-to-room basis eventually completing the entire house. When the last room is completed, the cycle will be started over, enabling a thorough inspection and maintenance in each year. In some smaller properties, Bosspitality _ might be a part-time assignment for a maintenance man and scheduled on a weekly basis. Since the principle of the cart is to avoid traveling back and forth between shop and rooms, a specific time each week should be set aside for stocking the cart to eliminate needless trips. Equipment to be carried in the cart includes a comprehensive checklist and all tools and materials necessary for room maintenance.

Bosspitality _ should be an all-round mechanic and as such requires training. Since Bosspitality _ probably has more guest contact than anyone else in the Engineering Department, the person chosen should be carefully selected. Do not block out the idea of a female Bosspitality _ in selecting a responsible person for this position. The first day the Chief Engineer should go through several rooms completely with Bosspitality _ showing him what to look for. During the first weeks, each trade should spend at least a few hours training Hospitality _. The electrical shop may want to show him the location of the breaker panels and the proper tripping and resetting procedure, how to replace receptacles and light switches, safety precautions, etc.

The locksmith should instruct Hospitality _ in the removal, disassembly, repair, and/or replacement of guest room locks. A paper hanger may show him how to re-glue, replace and repair vinyl wall covering. Other trades should instruct Hospitality _ in his duties until he can perform all phases of the work required. Not to be overlooked during the training period is proper personal appearance and guest relations.

Hospitality _ is responsible for leaving the guest room in perfect condition. Any deficiency that will take an excessive amount of time to correct or is beyond Hospitality Fix it capabilities should be noted on a Work Request Ticket immediately. Such items may include upholstery and furniture repair, burn holes in carpet, painting of walls and television repair, etc. Tickets written on minor items should be turned in the next

time Hospitality _ is in the engine room. Tickets written on major deficiencies should be telephoned in for more speedy repair. This procedure is thoroughly covered by the WORK REQUEST SYSTEM.

A quota system has been developed where 25% of the guest rooms are serviced each month by Hospitality It: i.e. , four months should see all guest rooms receive the Hospitality treatment. For Bosspitalityit purposes, a year consists of three periods each containing four months or eighty working days. Twenty working days make a month while five working days constitute a week.

A comprehensive list of duties should be in the cart. This checklist is an in-house reporting and reference system. Each item is checked off as inspected and/or repaired. A sample checklist is included which should be customized to your specific needs. At the end of each week the checklist is to be handled to the Chief Engineer. The checklist is to be filed by date for one year in the Chief Engineer's Office. At the end of the year these sheets should be placed in a binder and marked with the date and the words "Bosspitalityit".

At variable intervals, but not more than a week apart, the Chief Engineer should take along Hospitality and inspect a series of rooms freshly completed. Any deficiencies should be discussed at this time. It is suggested that at least ten percent of the rooms be inspected by the Chief Engineer in this manner. Rooms thus inspected should be set off with an asterisk on the Hospitality It Monthly Report, Figure 2.

Hotel: Name of the Property

Date: Date report is filled out.

Period: Period I

Period

Period III

No. of Rooms: The total number of guest rooms.

Monthly Quota: The total number of rooms to be inspected by Hospitality It for the month. A one-thousand room hotel would have a quota of 1000/80 - 12.5 rooms per day, 12.5 x 5 = 62.5 rooms per week, or 62.5 x 4 = 250 rooms per month. (25% of total number of rooms).

Completed This Month: This means the total number of rooms that Hospitality It Man has completed that particular month.

% This Month: To arrive at the percentage, divide the number of completed rooms by the quota for that month, multiply by 100.

Completed This Period: The total number of rooms that Hospitality It has completed in a particular period.

% This Period: Calculation is similar to the % This Month, where it is the completed this period" figure divided by "No. of Rooms". In other words, the 1000 room hotel at the end of the second month of that particular period, should have completed 500 rooms. Therefore, his% This period would be 500/1000 = 50%.

Number of rooms inspected by Chief Engineer: Total number of rooms that have been inspected this month by the Chief Engineer after completion by Hospitality It. Set off these room numbers below with an asterisk.

% This Month: Percentage of rooms checked by Chief Engineer. Divide the number of rooms inspected by the Chief Engineer by the number of rooms completed by Hospitality It.

Hospitality-IT MAINTENANCE CHECKLIST

AIR CONDITIONERS
1. Pneumatic Control - (Lubricate valve stem & O-ring, check opening and closing)
2. Knob on Thermostat - (Secure)
3. Filter - (Clean)
4. Condense Water Drain - (Clean)
5. Hand Valves - (Check, to be open) LAMPS (PORTABLE)
6. Switches - (Check)
7. Lamp Socket - (Tighten)
8. Lamp Shades - (Repair or Replace)
9. Cord on Valance Light Pull Switch (Check, replace if necessary)
10. Cover on Valance Light - (Secure)
11. Bulb - (Replace if necessary)
12. Plugs - (Replace if necessary)

SWITCHES AND RECEPTACLES
13. Outlet Wall Plates - (Change plates to match wall color, inspect, clean, secure)
14. Switches - Change plates to match wall color, inspect, clean secure)
15. Switches & Receptacles - (Replace missing screws)
16. Receptacles - Change if necessary)

TELEVISIONS
17. Audio (Check radio channels)
18. Video (Check television channels)
19. Knobs (Replace if necessary)
20. Fine Tuning (Adjust if necessary)
21. Antenna Outlet (Secure plate)
22. Antenna Connectors (Check, repair if necessary)
23. Remote Control and Connections (Check)

TELEPHONE
24. Dialing Instructions (Replace if necessary or broken)
25. Defects (Report any other defects to hotel operator).

FURNITURE
26. Drawer Handles & Knobs (Check, replace, if necessary)
27. Drawer Guides (Lubricate if needed with FET)
28. Stains (Clean and Touch up)
29. Springs on Chairs (Check)
30. Marble Table Tops (Check, repair small defects)
31. Headboards (Check and secure)
32. Wheels (Check and secure)
33. Window Casters (Lubricate with FET)

WINDOWS AND MIRRORS
34. Mirror Hangers (Check and secure)
35. Window Hardware (Check and secure)

DRAPERY TRACK AND ROLLERS
36. Inspect and secure all drapery track and rollers.

CLOSETS
37. Sliding Door Tracks (Check and repair if necessary)
38. Floor Guides for Sliding Doors (Check)
39. Bumpers on Sliding Doors (Check)
40. Floor Door Stop (Check)
41. Wall Hooks (Check)

DOORS (MAIN ENTRANCE, BATHROOM AND CONNECTING)
42. Handles (Check)
43. Lock Cylinder Set Screw (Check)
44. Hinges and Hinge Pins (Lubricate with **FET** and Secure)
45. Door Chain (Check, repair if necessary)
46. Lock Striker Plates (Check and secure)
47. Night Latch (Check)
48. Door Frame Rubber Bumpers (Check, replace if necessary)
49. Fire Exit Plan (Check)

BATHROOM
50. Bathtubs Safety - Slip Guard used.
51. Toilet **Flush** Valve (Check)
52. Toilet Cover Bumper (Check)
53. Seat Hinges (Check and Secure)
54. Toilet Seal (Check for evidence of leaks)
55. Bath Drain Plugs & Pop-Up (Check)
56. Mixing Valve (Secure Handles)
57. Mixing Valve Washers (Replace if necessary)
58. Hot and Cold Faucets (Check and/or replace "H" and "C" buttons)
59. Escutcheon Plates (Secure)
60. Shower Enclosure, Tracks and Doors (Check)
61. Shower Enclosure Bumpers and Handles (Check)
62. Ice Water Mechanism (Check)
63. P Trap under basin (Check)
64. Drain Pop-Ups (Check)
65. Faucet Strainer (Clean and Replace)
66. Basin Bowl Hangers (Re-glue or resecure)
67. Toilet Paper Holder (Check)
68. Razor Blade Dispenser (Check)
69. Bottle Opener (Check)
70. Kleenex Holder (Replace or Re Secure)
71. Floor and Wall Tile (Check)
72. Soap Dish and Grab Bars (Check and Secure)
73. Towel Racks (Resecure)
74. Toilet Privacy Locks (Check)

BATHROOM SCALES
- 75. Check correct weight
- 76. Check mechanism under scales

GENERAL CHECK
- 77. **Baseboards** (Check)
- 78. Carpet (Check)
- 79. Vinyl (Check)
- 80. Pictures (Check)
- 81. Ceiling (Check for cracks and/or peeling paint)
- 82. Paint (Check paint on walls and door casings)

MAINTENANCE CART IN ACTION

Mounted Equipment

Showing is

CUSTOMER

Applied to

Middi Model

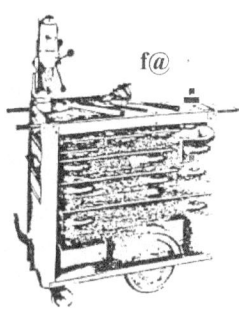

SPECIFICATION- MIDDI MODEL - Std. color, maintenance orange black drawers.

18" x 36" Top - 1/ 8" Masonite overlay - 37" high. 11

various size drawers - 1 1/2" x 1" modular.

Total Locking Front Cover - **Shown** recessed.

12 Small Parts Pockets - each end.
12 x 2" Polyurethane Main Wheels - AND / H Ball Bearings.

5" x 1-5 / 8" POLY - on Nylon Casters.

Floor Brake - Chrome hardware.
Body - 1 6 - 18 gauge Steel - Wt. 234 lbs. 10

years structural guarantee.

Optional colors and Drawer choice available.

Baby buggy balance to walk over door sills, elevator cracks, steps and other obstructions. Designed for smooth, easy rolling - heavily loaded - over carpeted floors.

OTHERS SIZES - SAME SPECIFICATIONS -
18" X 28" Top - 8 DRAWER -   JUNIOR MODEL
18" X 44" Top - 14 DRAWER -   UTILITY MODEL
24" x 44" Top- 14 DRAWER-   SENIOR MODEL

ROLL- ON....

....the only carts with the easy rolling big wheel and famous baby-buggy balances.

Hospitality IT MONTHLY SUMMARY REPORT

Hotel _____ Date _____
No. of Rooms _____ Monthly Quota _____
Completed this month   % this month ___
Completed this month   % this period ___
No. of rooms inspected by
    Chief Engineer ____ %this month ___

COMPLETED ROOM NUMBERS

_____ _____ _____ _____ _____ _____ _____ _____
_____ _____ _____ _____ _____ _____ _____ _____
_____ _____ _____ _____ _____ _____ _____ _____
_____ _____ _____ _____ _____ _____ _____ _____
_____ _____ _____ _____ _____ _____ _____ _____
_____ _____ _____ _____ _____ _____ _____ _____
_____ _____ _____ _____ _____ _____ _____ _____
_____ _____ _____ _____ _____ _____ _____ _____
_____ _____ _____ _____ _____ _____ _____ _____
_____ _____ _____ _____ _____ _____ _____ _____
_____ _____ _____ _____ _____ _____ _____ _____
_____ _____ _____ _____ _____ _____ _____ _____

LEGEND
Period I January 1 - April 30
Period II May 1 - August 31
Period III September 1 - December 31
Engineering Operations
470 Atlantic Avenue
Boston 10, Mass. 02210

NOTES
1. syndicate rooms inspected by Chief Engineer by *.
2. Repons must be mailed no later than 11 15* of each month.
Chief Engineer ___

IU 2E

PROPERTY OPERATIONS POLICIES AND PROCEDURES

Subject:	**Hospitality-IT** Section: PROGRAMS

PURPOSE: Promo the guest satisfaction by ensuring that guest rooms and public are maintained in excellent condition and in working order.

POLICY: The Chief Engineer is to implement and maintain the Hospitality program.

STANDARDS:
1. A Hospitality mobile maintenance earl will be stocked with required spare parts and materials and appropriate hand tools for daily use by the Hospitality Mechanic.
2. The Hospitality Mechanic will inventory the cart weekly.
3. The Hospitality It checklists will be used for guest rooms and public area.
4. 25 percent of all guest rooms will be inspected and deficiencies corrected monthly.
5. All public areas will be inspected and deficiencies corrected monthly.
6. The Chief Engineer is to inspect 10 percent of the completed Hospitality guest rooms and the public areas monthly.
7. The Hospitality Summary Report will be completed monthly.

PROCEDURE
1. Each property is to purchase mobile maintenance cart to be used as a portable workshop/tool bench. The cart must have the following characteristics:

   c. Large wheels to allow mobility over carpets, door sills and in and out of elevators.

   e. Am ple storage space such as drawers and parts pockets. so that it can be organized for maximum efficiency.

   g. Locks to prevent theft of parts and materials.

   i. A brake so that it remains stationary when used as a workbench.

   k. Approximate size of the cart is to be 45 cm (W) x 90 (L) x 95 (H).

2. The Hospitality earl is to be stocked with spare parts and materials that typically would be used to maintain the guest rooms and public areas.

Subject: Hospitality-IT	Section PROGRAMS	Number: 2.1	Page 2 of 12

3. It is the responsibility of the Hospitality Mechanic to inventory the cart weekly to ensure that it is fully stocked and to advise the Chief Engineer of parts and materials that needs to be purchased as inventories are depleted.
4. The Hospitality It tool list, as in Figure I, is to be used as a guideline in purchasing the necessary hand tools which are to be maintained on the cart.
5. The Chief Engineer must develop a comprehensive Hospitality It Checklist for the rooms and public areas. Examples of checklists are shown in Figure 2 and 3. These examples are to be used as a guidelines in developing checklists tailored specifically to your hotel.
6. A monthly quota of 25 percent (minimum) or the guest rooms must be completed. The quota will ensure that every guest room is completed three(3) times per year.
7. The Hospitality Mechanic is to be use a Maintenance Check List for each room and check mark each item inspected and/or repaired.
8. The guest contact areas to be inspected monthly. The Hospitality Mechanic will use a Public Area Maintenance Checklist and check mark each item inspected and/or repaired.
9. As a rule of thumb, one full-time Hospitality Mechanic is required per 500 rooms. This position is a full-time position; therefore, the Hospitality Mechanic is not to be used for other work unless in an emergency situation.
10. At the start of each week, the Chief Engineer will provide the Hospitality Mechanic with a list of rooms to be completed. The rooms which have been completed are to be tracked to ensure that there is no duplication of rooms (until the entire hotel has been completed).
11. An y noted deficiency requiring an excessive amount of time to repair, or beyond the Hospitality Mechanics ability is to be noted on a work request ticket and returned to the Chief Engineer. Major problems are to be telephoned in to the Engineering Department to ensure that they are handled expeditiously.
12. It is the Hospitality It Mechanic's responsibility to leave the room cleaned in perfect order after completion of any work performed.
13. The Chief Engineer is to inspect 10 percent (minimum) to the recently completed guest rooms and all public areas throughout the course of each month. Any deficiencies noted are to be brought to the attention of the Hospitality Mechanic. This will help to ensure that the program is working properly and identify further training needs.
14. At the end of each week the Hospitality Mechanic is to provide the Chief Engineer with the completed Checklists. At the end or each month the completed public area Checklist must be submitted.
15. At the end of each month the Chief Engineers to complete the Hospitality Summary Report as in Figure 4. A copy of the report must be maintained on file.

| Subject: Hospitality-IT | Section PROGRAMS | Number: 2.1 | Page 3 of 12 |

FIGURE 1. - Hospitality IT TOOL GUIDELINE

Description

Set of typical Hand Tools/Pouch 110 mm Vise (mount on top of cart) 40 mm Wood Wallpaper Roller
Set (4) Nail Sets
250 mm Bastard Cut Flat File/Handle 350mm Flat Mill File/Handle
250 mm Putty Knife
150 mm Block Plane Awl
3/8" Drive Ratchet
17mm Deep Well Socket (12pt) 13mm Deep Well Socket
10mm Deep Well Socket
25 mm Nylon Paintbrush
50 mm China Bristle Paint Brush Artist Paint Brushes (assorted) 200 mm **Drywall** Knife
3/8" Cordless Drill Hacksaw/Blades Keyhole Saw
Caulking Gun/Tub Caulk
10 m Flat Extension Cord Oil can
Picture Tool (s)
TV Cable Security Tool
TV "Box" Programming Tool
VolVO ohm Multimeter Digital Thermometer Wire Strippers
Utility Knife Carpet Scissors
Portable Vacuum Cleaner

Subject: Hospitality-I	Section PROGRAMS	Number: 2.1	Page 4 of 12

FIGURE 2. - Hospitality GUEST ROOM CHECKLIST GUIDELINE

1. **ENTRY**

    Door Condition/Appearance Lock Operation
    Night Latch Security Latch
    Door Closer/Hinges
    Door Bumper Door Viewer
    Emergency Evacuation Signage
    Security Signage Wall covering
    Baseboard/Cove
    Carpet
    Ceiling
    Ceiling Light
    Light Switch And Cover
    Threshold
    Rate Card/Holder

21. **CLOSET**

    Door Condition/Appearance Door Track
    Shelf A GO Rod
    Wall covering
    Baseboard/Cove
    Carpet
    Ceiling Ceiling Light
    Light Switch and Cover
    Tie Rack

34. **BATHROOM**

    Door Condition/Appearance Door Operation
    Door Hardware/Hinges
    Door Bumper Robe Hook
    Vanity Condition/Appearance
    Mirror
    Light Fixture/Bulbs Light Switch/Cover
    GFCI Receptacle and Cover
    Sink
    Sink Faucet/Aerator
    Sink valves/Stopper Water Temperature Water Pressure Towel Bars

Subject: Hospitality-IT	Section PROGRAMS	Number: 2.1	Page 5 of 12

Make-up Mirror
Hair Dryer
Television
Telephone
Tissue Dispenser(s)
Bottle Opener
Tub(Non-slip
Tub Feet Vh1/Stopper
Shower Head
Soap Dishes
Wall Tile/Grout
Toilet Seat
Toilet Ballcock/Water Level
Wall Covering
Baseboard/Cove
Floor Covering
Ceiling
Exhaust GlUe
Threshold
Grab Bar secure

22. **BEDROOM**

Ceil Ng
Wallcovering
Baseboard/Cove
Carpet
Connect11,g Doo,Condition/Appearance
Connecth,g Ouo, Lock Operation
Connect111g DoorHinges, Window Condition/Appearance, Drape Operation/Hardware
A/C Unit Condell on/Appearance
A/C Operation/T Stat Setting
A/C Filters
A/C Drah, Pan
A C Grille (s)
Bed Frame/Headboard
Tables, Desk,Chairs Condition
Dresser/Armoire Condition
Sofa Condition
Night Stand Condition
Table Lamp (s) Switch/Shade/Bulb/Plug, Floor Lamps (s) Swatch/Shade/Bulb/Plug, Radio/TV Operation/Plug (s)
Light Switch (s) Cover (s)
Outlets a,,dCovers
Telephone Operation/Jack
Mirrors
Artwork
Alarm Clock/Correct Time

71

| Subject: Hospitality-IT | Section PROGRAMS | Number: 2.1 | Page 6 of 12 |

1. WET BARS

Cabinet Co11dition/Appear 11ce
Countertop Con d iti on /Apple
ara11ce Sink Condition/appearance
Sink Faucet Valves Operation/Appearance
Ceiling
Ceiling Fixture/Bulbs
Light Switch/Cover
GFI/Outlet/Cover
Wall-covering

Baseboard/Cove
Floor covering
Refrigerator Operating/Temperature
Coffee Maker/Plug

17. LIFE SAFETY

Smoke Detector/Operation
Em erg e11cy Speaker
Sprinkler Head (s)

Subject: Hospitality-I	Section PROGRAMS	Number: 2.1	Page 7 of 12

FIGURE 3. - Hospitality PUBLIC AREA CHECKLIST GUIDELINE

1. **GUEST ROOM CORRIDORS**

   Door Frames, Room Numbers, Wallcovering, BtTeebo"in fiCove, Floor covering, Ceiling
   HVAC Grilles
   Light Fixtures, Bulbs
   Signage
   Outlet/Cover Plates
   Wall King Area, FIORP Covering
   Vending Area, Walls/Ceiling, Ice Machine
   Sod ITM hine, Cord Draw, Smoke Detectors
   Fire Alarm Speakers/S. Sprinkler Heads
   Pull Stations
   Exhaust & Fire Duct, Smoke Purge, Supply ing
   Bh11fb DoorsCondition

2. **ELEVATOR FOYERS**

   Ceiling, Wallcovering, Base Tr, Trolley, Floor Covering
   ight Fixtures Bl nhl
   Exit Light
   Signage
   Doors and frames
   Fire System Devices, ArtWork, Advertising, Telephone
   Furniture
   Smoke Detector, Sprinkler Heads
   Info. Safety Sign

43. **ELEVATOR CABS**

   Floor Covering
   Wall Treatm'nt/HiMwork
   Ceiling
   Lighting
   Emergency Telephone, Floor/Level/or Panel, Cl15 Numbers

53. **LOBBY/CIRCULATION AREA**

   Ceiling, Wallcovering, Base, Trim Kore
   Floor Covering

73

| Subject: **Hospitality-IT** | Section PROGRAMS | Number: 2.1 | Page 8 of 12 |

Light Switches/Cover Plates
Outlets/Cover Plates Windows
Drapery Operation/Hardware
Millwork
Furniture
Artwork
Dooors/Door Frames
Door Hardware JH Iunges /Co sure
Signage
Telephones
Exit Signs
Smoke Detectors
Fire Alarm/Speakers
Pull Station Sprinkler
Heads

18. FRONT DESK AREA

Ceiling
Wall covering
Baseboard/Cove
FLOor Covering
Light Fixtures/Bulbs
Light Switches/Cover Plates
Outlets Cover Plates
Desk Top
Millwork
Drawer/Door Operation
Door (s)/Door Frame (s)
Door Hardware/Hinges/Closure
Telephones
All Signs
Sprinkler Heads
Fire Alarm/Speakers
Smoke Detectors
Hold Up Alarm

6. BUSINESS CENTER

Ceiling
Wall covering
Baseboard/
Cove FLOor
Covering
Light Fixtures/Bulbs
Light Switch (s)/Cover Plates (s)
Outlets/Cover Plates
Millwork/ Furniture
Equipment
Telephone
Door/Door Frame
Door Hardware/Hinges/Closure
Smoke Detector
Sprinkler Heads Fire
Alarm/Speakers

74

Subject: **Hospitality-IT**	Section **PROGRAMS**	Number: 2.1	Page 9 of 12

1. LOUNGE (S)

   Ceiling
   Wall covering, Ri1seboa1d/Cove, Floor Covering, Millwork
   Furniture
   Light Fixtures/Bulbs
   Light Switches/CoverPlates, Outlets/CoverPlates
   Guest Room(s), Television(s), Telephone(s)
   Art Work
   Signage
   Smoke Detectors
   Fire Alarm/Spec Krim
   Exit Signs

8. RESTAURANTS

   Ceiling
   Wall covering, Ri1seboa1d/Cove, Floor Covering, Millwork
   Furniture
   Light Fixtures/VS bulbs
   Light Switches/CoverPlates, Outlets/CoverPlates, Signage
   Art Work, Sprinkler Heads
   Smoke Detectors, Fire All Lou/Speakers, Exit Signs

9. GIFT SHOP

   Ceiling
   Wall covering, Ri1seboa1d/Cove, Floor Covering
   Light Switches/CoverPlates, Outlets/CoverPlates, Equipment
   Millwork
   Smoke Detectors
   Fire All/Lou/Speakers
   Sprinkler Heads

10. MEETING ROOMS

    Ceiling
    Wallcover1ork
    Ri1seboa1d/Cove, Floor Covering
    Light Fixtures/Bulbs
    Light Switches/CoverPlates

75

Subject: Hospitality-IT	Section PROGRAMS	Number: 2.1	Page 10 of 12

Outlet Slipcover Pb1es
Ocевary Operation/Hardware With
DoomD 001/v am ell
DoorHeحdware/Hinge/Closure
Pocke t Wath Ea nd LHe
M llw o r h
Pub/ l Address Sect LA t !"
AK Outlet/Cover Pl1tes s
Exit Signs
Sprinkler Heads Fire Alarm/Fixtures Smoke Detectors
Dimmers/Opc11Nvor

17. PUBLIC RESTROOMS

Door OperationFIlCopd Ble n/l 000THt n dw tl e/Hinge s/Closure Ceiling
W ll cove I t e/9
8 iiseboa1 BCove
Floor Covering
Ligh t LF y tures/Bulb
Light Switch (plates) PHD 2/
Outle ts/Cover Pkl1e /7
But tl Pa tt itions/I L ellw Re
Toilet Operations/Hostlward Urinals Operations/Fixtures Threshold
Tissue Holders
Grab B ars
Sink Countertop
Faucet/Ascrss/Valves/Stoppe nt
Pittpcr Tower Dispenser Pitpcr Towel Receptacle
Soap Dispensers
Mirror
Fu rn itur e
Millwork
Sprinkler Heads
Fire Alarm Speakers

45. POOL AREA

Door (s) Condition/Appearance Door (s) Himhh11a Hinges/Closure
Ceiling W 11cove ring
Base bo .11o Cove
Deck
Light Fixtures/Bulbs
Light Switch (es)Cover P tes (s) Outlet Cover Plates
Furniture Mllwork
Telep hon Ince Switch PBX
Safety Signage Safety Equipment

Subject: **Hospitality-IT**	Section PROGRAMS	Number: 2.1	Page 11 of 12

Exit Signs, Smoke Detectors, Sprinkler Heads
Fire Alarm/Speakers
Gate/Self Closing

7. **HEALTH CLUB**

Door (s) Operation/Appearance, Door (s) Hardware/Hinges/ Closure, Ceiling
wall covering
Baseboard /Cove, Floor Covering, Light Fixtures/Bulbs
Light Switch Cover Plate
Outlets/Cover Plates
Equipment, Telephone/Dir ct, Switch PBX, Safety Signage
Lockers
Shower Stall Wall Tile/Grout
Shower Head
Shower Valve/Soap Dishes, Shower Curtain Rod
Stall Partitions/Hardware
Urinal Operation/Hardware, Sink Countertop
Sink Faucet/Aerator/Valves/Stoppers, Drains
Exit Signs
Sprinkler Heads, Smoke Detectors, Fire Alarm/Sprinkler

Subject: Hospitality-IT	Section PROGRAMS	Number: 2.1	Page 12 of 12

FIGURE 3 - Hospitality IT SUMMARY REPORT

Hospitality IT MONTHLY SUMMARY REPORT

Hot e l _____ Date _Peir d_ _____
Number of Rooms _____ Mohyl Quota _____

Completed this month ___ %this month
Colmdtispedrio%hispeird ___ N.ofRooms inspected ___ % this month ___

COMPLETED ROOM NUMBERS

_____ _____ _____ _____ _____ _____ _____ _____ _____ _____
_____ _____ _____ _____ _____ _____ _____ _____ _____ _____
_____ _____ _____ _____ _____ _____ _____ _____ _____ _____
_____ _____ _____ _____ _____ _____ _____ _____ _____ _____
_____ _____ _____ _____ _____ _____ _____ _____ _____ _____
_____ _____ _____ _____ _____ _____ _____ _____ _____ _____
_____ _____ _____ _____ _____ _____ _____ _____ _____ _____
_____ _____ _____ _____ _____ _____ _____ _____ _____ _____
_____ _____ _____ _____ _____ _____ _____ _____ _____ _____
_____ _____ _____ _____ _____ _____ _____ _____ _____ _____
_____ _____ _____ _____ _____ _____ _____ _____ _____ _____
_____ _____ _____ _____ _____ _____ _____ _____ _____ _____
_____ _____ _____ _____ _____ _____ _____ _____ _____ _____
_____ _____ _____ _____ _____ _____ _____ _____ _____ _____

LEGEND
Period I January 1 - April 30
Period II May 1 - August 30
Period III September 1 - December 31

Chief Engineer

NOTES
1. Indicate rooms inspected Chief Engineer by •.

PROPERTY OPERATIONS POLICIES AND PROCEDURES

Subject: **REPAIR** LOG ~~Section: PROGRAMS~~

PURPOSE:

To provide an equipment inventory index and cost breakdown history of all major equipme11L The Repair Log is to be used as the basis in determining if a piece of equipment should be repaired.

POLICY: The Chief Engi11eeris to develop a11d mai11tai11 the Repair Log Program.

STANDARDS:

1. A Repair Log Data Sheet will be completed for each piece of equipment serviced by the Department.
2. Replacement parts and labour repair costs associated with the repair of piece of equipment are to be recorded on the **Repair Log Record.**
3. A Master Copy of the **Repair Log Data** a11d **Record Sheets** will bemaintainedand kept curre11t.
4. The Repair Log is to be reviewed annually.

PROCEDURE

1. This policy is to be set up prior to developing the **Preventive Mainte 1,ance Program** as the information needed will be extracted from the Repair Log.
2. A list of all equipment serviced by the Property Operations Department is to be compiled.
3. A Repair Log Data Sheet as in Figure 1, is to be completed for each piece of equipment from the list referenced above.
4. The Repair Log Data Sheet Is completed as follows:

    Service - List service provided such as compressed air, exhaust domestic hot water, etc. Type

    Machine - Describe equipme11t, such as hot water boiler, supply fan, laundry dryer, etc.

    Equipment I.D. No. - The equipment identification number is taken from the Equipment Schedule which is developed in 1 accordance with the tag number system, as per figure 3.

    Location - Give the specific area in which the equipment is located, such as main mechanical room, roof, etc.

    Serial No. - List the serial number, as identified by the equipment manufacturer.
    Model No. - List the model number as identified by the equipment manufacturer.

    Make - The Name of the equipment manufacturer.

Subject:	Section	Number: 2.2	Page 2 of 10
REPAIR LOG	PROGRAMS		

Date Purchased - The Date the equipment was put into service (if available).
Purchase Cost - The equipment cost at the time of purchase (if available). Preventive

Maintenance Procedure - The functions and time intervals.

Function - The specific maintenance items are to be performed, as recommended and/or specified by the equipment manufacturer.

Interval - The corresponding maintenance time frames for each specific functions, such as weekly, monthly, etc.

Special Instructions - Instructions of a specific nature particular to the equipment; such as: caution, automatic start, fan controlled by fire alarm; electrical disconnect is located in adjacent room; supply fan is interlocked with the exhaust fan and both must be restarted, etc.

1. Specifications - All applicable data pertaining to the equipment, such as Voltage

- voltage in volts.

Amperage - Current in amps.

Phase - Number of phase.

Pressure - Operating pressure in pascals. Horsepower -

Power developed expressed as HP.

RPM - Revolutions per minute.
Drive - The method of power transmission such ass belt, gear, direct. Belts -

The size and number.

Fuse - Type and size
Lubrication - Type oil, grease, etc. as specified by the equipment manufacturer. Filters -

Type and number.

Fluids - The working fluid of the system such as hydraulic oil, refrigerant 22, etc.

Note: When complex machinery is involved, it may be necessary to list additional informaL\ n on the back of the Repair Log Data Sheet. An example would be a laundry washer using both a primary and secondary drive system. In this case, primary specifications should be listed on the

Subject:	Section	Number: 2.2	Page 3 of 10
REPAIR LOG	PROGRAMS		

The front page, and the information concerning secondary system on the back page. It is of utmost importance to list as much information concerning the equipment specifications as possible.

5. A Repair Log Record Sheet, as in Figure 2, must be maintained for each piece of equipment for which a Repair Log Data sheet has been completed.

   Equipment 1.0. No. - The equipment tag number.

   Date - The date during which repairs were made.

   Work Performed - A description of work performed including parts and/or materials repaired and/or replaced.

   Hours - Total hours required to complete a repair.
   Materials - The cost of material and/or parts used to complete a repair. Labour -

   The labour cost associated with a repair.

   Cost to Date - The combined total cost to date for material and labour for all repairs completed.

7. The Repair Log Record Sheet is not to include costs associated with preventive maintenance. Ensure that all outside labour and materials are included in addition to in-house labour and materials.

8. It is recommended that the Repair Log Data sheets be inserted in clear plastic sheet protectors and stored in a three ring binder. The Repair log Record Sheet is to be kept adjacent to its companion data sheet within the binder.

9. The Repair Log is to be reviewed annually to determine the following:

   c. Effectiveness Of the Preventive Maintenance.

   e. Quality of replacement parts.
   g. Potential for equipment replacement due to the cost breakdown history. The above procedures pertain to any new equipment purchased.

10.

11. If the department has a personal computer or access to one, it is recommended that the Repair Log System to be computerized using the Chief Software.

Subject:	Section	Number: 2.2	Page 4 of 10
REPAIR LOG	PROGRAMS		

FIGURE 1. - REPAIR LOG DATA SHEET

Service	Type Machine	Equipment
Location	Serial No.	Model No.
Make	Date Purchased	Purchased Cost

PREVENTIVE MAINTENANCE PROCEDURE

Function	Interval

SPECIAL INSTRUCTIONS

SPECIFICATIONS

Voltage	Drive
Amperage	Belts
Phase	Fuse
Cycle	Threads/Hour
Horsepower	Filter
RPM	Fluids

Subject:	Section	Number: 2.2
REPAIR LOG	PROGRAMS	

FIGURE 2. - REPAIR LOG RECORD SHEET

Date	By	Work Performed	Hours	Cost Materials	Cost Labour	Cost To date

Subject:	Section	Number: 2.2	
REPAIR LOG	PROGRAMS		

FIGURE 3. - IDENTIFYING OF EQUIPMENT FOR PREVENTIVE MAINTENANCE

The equipment number called the TAG NO is a 7 digit code which is used to identify a particular piece of equipment.

The **TAG NO** is divided into three sets of codes as described below.

All equipment in the hotel must be labelled with TAG NO, and strongly recommended to fix a permanent tag to the equipment such as plast or alu labels, but note that paintings or stickers are alternative means for some applications.

Hotels with existing number system, which vary from the TAG NO, can be left with their system, but hotels which will install computerized maintenance systems have to convert to the new TAG NO SYSTEM.

A chart code has been developed which is divided into 10n types of maintenance records as follows:

1. TERRAIN AND BUILDING
2. FOOD AND BEVERAGE EQUIPMENT
3. AIR CONDITIONING
4. TRANSPORT EQUIPMENT
5. STEAM WATER AND GAS
6. ELECTRICAL INSTALLATIONS
7. VARIOUS EQUIPMENT
8. FIRE AND SAFETY EQUIPMENT
9. GUEST ROOMS
10. ENGINEERING ADMINISTRATION.

Il is essential that the equipment is divide into the above-mentioned types in order to maintain a uniform system throughout the division, thereby making support and reporting easier.

The numbers used for each type of maintenance records are recommendation and can be adjusted to match the individual application.

The first 3 digits of the TAG NO is a numeric code used to identify what type of equipment it is, e.g. the sprinkler pump will be type 810, the coffee machine in the restaurant type 260, the cooling tower type 350 and the drilling machine in the workshop type 740, etc.

The next set of codes is a two digit alphanumeric code used to identify on which floor the equipment is located, e.g. 14 is on the 14"' floor, 81 could be basement 1, RT could be the roof top and CP could identify the car park.

The third and last section of the TAG NO is a two digit code used as a serial number to separate this particular equipment from all other, e.g. 01 is the first equipment of this type on this floor while 02 will be the next, etc.

Subject:	Section	Number: 2.2	Page 7 of 10
REPAIR LOG	PROGRAMS		

A power panel on the second floor will be labeled as follows:

    640   for the type
    02   for the location
    01   for the first panel.

Putting all together the TAG NO for this panel will be 640-02-01. In case there are two panels on the same floor the next panel would be 640-02-02, etc.

For hotels which use - 1, etc. to describe the first basement a slash can be used as separator for the TAG NO (250/-1/01).

The total outline of the system is described on the following page together with a sample list.

Subject: **REPAIR** LOG	Section PROGRAMS	Number: 2.2

MAINTENANCE RECORD TYPES FOR USE WITH ANY MAINTENANCE SOFTWARE

TYPE	1 TERRAIN & BUILDING	TYPE	6 Electrical INSTALLATION
110	Doors	810	Emergency Supply
120	Keys & locks	820	811 Lifters & Ch 11 Rgc 1
130	Surface outside	830	Substation
140	Surface inside	840	Power un of 110,1 fon - 08.8o 11nd
150	Loose Furniture	850	Light Outdoor
160	Bedd'le furniture	860	Light Indoor
170	Signs	870	TV & Video
180	Ocont II tion Windows & Mirrors	880	PA & Sm/11BP ower
190	G11rd on, Ro11d, W11ks A.P lay # 81 . lot	890	Telephone Sys fent
199	Other Terrain & Building	899	Other Electric,11
TYPE	2 FOOD & SEVERAGE	TYPE	7 VARIOUS EQUIPMENT
210	Cooking & Proocu/g in, used 11 htm	710	Health Club Equipment
220	Ice Cubers & P111/to 1s	720	Laundry Equipment
230	Oven & Convection 11o	730	Housekee u/71Equipm/ht
240	R11nge Grill Fire Grill	740	Tool m&a Workshop Equipment
250	Dish /Glass Washers	750	Air Compressors
260	Coffee Machine	760	Banquet Equipment n
270	Cuter Sm/11"cs, et .	770	
280	R c K u n C bled Counters	780	
290	Mixers Ice C1o 11m & teams	790	
299	Other Food & Beverage	799	Other V111t wv s Equipment
TYPE	3 AIR CONDITIONING	TYPE	8 FIRE & SAFETY EQUI PIE H A T
310	Am, ve it ors	810	Sprinklder & Fire W11dc 1 Smoke ExhTluct
320	Elbow/Stunds	820	A1111 fn Sys 1 em
330	Chillers	830	
340	Chilled Water in 8 11 1 1100	840	H1 3o n & CO 2
350	Cooing Tr for er	850	system Hose Reel
360	Heating H1d 01 tion	860	Fire Extinguisher
370	P11ain gc Unit s	870	
380	Boilers	880	
390	Pumps	890	
399	Other Air Condition	899	Other Fire S 1ef ty

Subject:	Section	Number: 2.2	Page 9 of 10
REPAIR LOG	PROGRAMS		

MAINTENANCE RECORD TYPES FOR USE WITH ANY MAINTENANCE SOFTWARE

TYPE	11 TRANSPORT EQUIPMENT
410	Guest Lift
420	Service Lift
430	Pallet Trucks, Trolley
440	Compressor
450	Pallet de Lift
460	Est lifter
470	Vehicle
490	Other Transport

TYPE	9 GUESTROOM
910	Fan Coil & Bathroom Appliances
920	TV & Radio
930	
940	Minibar
950	
960	
970	
980	
990	Other GuestROOm

TYPE	5 STEAM WATER & GAS
510	Steam in shot room
520	Water in act in room
530	Public BathRoom
540	Sewage Skimmer
550	Swimming Pool Fountain
560	Irrigation Inst
570	Heat Inst Gas hold room
580	Of fit B 111 ion
590	
599	Other Steam, Water & Gas

TYPE	10 ENGINEERING ADMINISTRATION
1010	BOMS
1020	Computer system
1030	Daily Routines
1040	Shift Routines
1050	Drawings
1060	Documentation
1070	
1080	
1090	
1099	Other Administration

Subject:	Section	Number: 2.2	
REPAIR LOG	PROGRAMS		

MAINTENANCE RECORDS - SAMPLES

170-GF-01	Neon Sign Main Entrance
190-GF-01	Car Park
220-14-01	Ice Cuber 14" Guest Floor
220-GF-01	Ice Cuber Main Kitchen No 1
260-TO-02	Coffee Machine Tower Lounge
310-B2-01	Air Handler for Laundry
310-B2-02	Air Handler

PROPERTY OPERATIONS POLICIES AND PROCEDURES

Subject: PREVENTIVE MAINTENANCE   Section: PROGRAM S

PURPOSE: To reduce downtime by minimizing mechanical failure, reduce operating costs by improving efficiency, extend the life of the equipment and maintain safety conditions.

POLICY: The Chief Engineer is to develop and maintain the Preventive Maintenance Program for all equipment not covered by a maintenance service contract.

STANDARDS:
1. Each piece of equipment is to be serviced in accordance with the manufacturer's specifications and local conditions.
2. Preventive Maintenance functions are to be entered on the Preventive Maintenance Weekly Schedule Sheets and spread equally over a 52 week period, so that maintenance is performed every week.
3. Preventive Maintenance Weekly Schedule Sheets are to be signed by the Engineering mechanic, dated and filed as proof of program compliance.

PROCEDURE
1. In order to ensure that each piece of equipment is serviced according to the manufacturer's specifications, the Repair Log must be completed prior to developing the Preventive Maintenance Program.
2. From the Repair log, compile a list of all equipment, respective equipment identification numbers, preventive maintenance functions and time intervals. This information is to be entered on the spreadsheet shown as Figure 1.
3. It is important that the work load is spread equally over a 52-week period, so that preventive maintenance is performed every week. By shifting the function time intervals horizontally, excessive work loads can be avoided. The number of spreadsheets required is determined by the property size and the number of pieces of equipment included within the preventive maintenance schedule. See example Spreadsheet as in Figure 2.
4. When the spread sheets have been completed and reworked to maximum efficiency, the Weekly Schedule Sheets. Shown as Figure 3, can be completed.
5. Each piece of equipment to be serviced on week one (1) is taken from the Spreadsheet and entered on a Weekly Schedule Sheet. Equipment name, Identification number and specific maintenance functions to be performed are to be entered. Week **two (2)** through **fifty-two (52)** are a week one necessary for most weeks. It is recommended that the completed Weekly Schedule Sheets be inserted in clear plastic sheet protectors, and the entire sheets are the **Master Sheet.** See example Weekly Schedule Sheets as in Figure **4.**

Subject:	Section	Number: 2.3	Page 2 of 6
PREVENTIVE MAINTENANCE	**PROGRAMS**		

6. Each week, the corresponding annual numerical Weekly Schedule Master Sheet is to be photocopied. This copy is to be called the Sub Master. The name of the employee responsible for completing the work is to be entered on the Sub-Master. Multiple copies of Sub-Masters may be required, which depends on the number of persons assigned to complete the work.

7. AS each piece of equipment is completed, the employee enters his or her initials and the date of completion on the Sub Master. Any additional work performed and/or needed is to be noted on the Sub-Master and a work request ticket written. The completed Sub-Master Weekly Schedule Sheet is then returned to the Chief Engineer, along with any work request tickets written.

8. The Chief Engineer is to review each returned Su-b Master sheet to ensure the Preventive Maintenance has been completed and to note any additional work performed or work which requires scheduling at a later date. Any Work performed above and beyond preventive maintenance is to be entered in the Repair Log Record.

9. The Sub Master are to be filed in a dated binder and retained for one year in the Engineering Office. At the end of this year, the binders are to be put in permanent storage and kept for legal purposes.

10. If the department has a personal computer or access to one. It is recommended that the preventive maintenance program be computerized using the Chief software.

| Subject: **PREVENTIVE MAINTENANCE** | Section **PROGRAMS** | Number: 2.3 | Page 3 of 6 |

FIGURE 1. - PREVENTIVE MAINTENANCE SPREADSHEET

EQUIPMENT I.D. NO.	WEEK NUMBER

| Subject: **PREVENTIVE MAINTENANCE** | Section **PROGRAMS** | Number: 2.3 | Page 4 of 6 |

FIGURE 2. - SPREADSHEET EXAMPLE

EQUIPMENT I.D. NO.	WEEK NUMBER
65 LB. Washer/Extractor #36-1a FLA	
125 lb. Washer/Extractor #42/24 FLA	
130 lb. Gas Dryer #L36C 042 C	
70 lb. Gas Dryer RL36C 036 G	
Utility Press #UR 47	
Compressor RP240	
Flatwork Ironer Maxima Plus 240	
Champion Dishwasher #U 20kb	
Southbend Fryer #3-6 944	
Southbend Range #424212	
Salamander Broiler #1	
Groen Oven/Steamer #M35	
Hobart Mixer #10975	
(Continue as Required)	97

| Subject: | Section | Number: 2.3 | Page 5 of 6 |
| **PREVENTIVE MAINTENANCE** | **PROGRAMS** | | |

FIGURE 3. - WEEKLY SCHEDULE SHEET   Week

Equipment & I.D. No.	MAINTENANCE FUNCTIONS	Assigned by	Completed by
			9

Record a11y other work performed or needed at a future date

Subject:	Section	Number: 2.3	Page 6 of 6
PREVENTIVE MAINTENANCE	PROGRAMS		

FIGURE 4. - WEEKLY SCHEDULE SHEET EXAMPLE   Week _ 1_

Equipment & I.D. No.	MAINTENANCE FUNCTIONS	Assigned by	Completed by
65lb. Washex # 36/18 FLA	Check: Programmer; Motor Mounts and Guard: Air Filter/Lubricator: ABLS.. Lubricator: Vee Belt Wear & Tension: Air Filter Element: Brake Lining.		
125lb Washex #42/24 FLA	Check: Repeat Above Steps		
Utility Press #UR-47	Check: Air FlLter-Clean 1l . Drain Tank-BlowDown.		
Compressor #F 240	Check: Oil Level: Air Receiver-Drai1.l Bell Tension; **Pulley and Pulley Set Screws**: Safety Valves-Test: Air Intake Filter-Clean Or Replace;Cooling Surfaces - Cle an intercooler, Aftercooler and compressor; Oil -for Contamination: Unloader. Unloader P.lot and Three-Way Valve.		
Ironer Max Plus 240	Check: Diameter of Pressinga Roll- Adjust: Co1w eeyore Belts - Tighten, Sprocket and Pulley Alignment 11l, Chains - Adjust a1l d Lubricate: Water Level: Burner Assembly; Vee Belts - Wear and Tension: Ironing Belts - Wear and Tear; Exhaust System - Clean: **Gearbox** Oil Level		
Southbend Ra1l ge #424212	Check : P.lot Flame - Clean and adjust; Burner- Clea11 a11d Adjust: Main Gas Valve - Clean and Confirm Con1l ection to Hood Suppression System.		
Hobart Mixer # 10073	Check: Planetary Oil Level: Transmission Oil Level: Slide Ways, **Lift Screw** a11d Hand Wheel Gear - Lubricate.		
	*Automatic Bearing Lubrication System		

Record a11v other work performed or needed at a future date

PROPERTY OPERATIONS POLICIES AND PROCEDURES

Subject:	FIRE PROTECTION PREVENTIVE MAINTENANCE	Section: PROGRAMS

PURPOSE: To provide a safe environment for hotel guest and employees, and to ensure the protection of hotel property and assets.

POLICY: The Chief Engineer is to develop and maintain a Fire Protection Preventive Maintenance Program as per Hospitality Hotels & Resorts Guidelines and applicable fire codes.

STANDARDS:

1. This program is to be maintained separately from the Preventive Maintenance Policy 2.3 (except properties using the Chief Software.

2. This program is to be implemented as per the Fire Protection Maintenance Schedule.

3. The Preventive Maintenance Policy 2.3 format will be used.

4. The complete Fire Protection Preventive Maintenance Schedule are to be filed in a dated binder for one year in the Chief Engineer's office. At the end of the year, the binders are to be put in permanent storage and kept for legal purposes.

PROCEDURE

1. An accurate list of all fire protection devices, including well defined locations, is to be compiled.

2. All applicable equipment and minimum equipment maintenance schedules, as in Figure 1, are to be incorporated and followed explicitly.

3. The list of General Tasks, as in Figure 2, is to be incorporated into the Fire Protection Preventive Maintenance Program.

4. The list to be used to complete the **Spreadsheet**, as explained in the Preventive Maintenance Policy 2.3 (See example spreadsheet **Figure 1**, Page 3 of 6, Preventive Maintenance Program 2, 3).

5. The Spreadsheet is to be completed so that the workload is spread equally over a 52-week period.

6. When the Spreadsheet is completed, the **Weekly Schedule Sheets** (See example shown in the Preventive Maintenance Policy 2.3, Figure 3, Page 5 of 6) are to be completed. Each device requiring Preventive Maintenance on wee (1) is taken from the Spreadsheet and entered on a Weekly Schedule Sheet. Device name, location and specific maintenance functions to be performed are entered. Weeks two (2) through fifty-two (52) are completed the same way. Multiple Weekly Schedule Sheets may be necessary.

Subject: FIRE PROTECTION PREVENTIVE MAINTENANCE	Section PROGRAMS	Number: 2.4	Page 2 of 7

It is recommended that the completed Weekly Schedule Sheets be inserted into clear plastic sheet protectors and the entire program stored in a three ring binder. These Sheets are the Master Sheets.

7. Each week the corresponding annual numerical Weekly Schedule Master Sheet is photocopied. This copy is referred to as the Sub Master. The name of the employee who is responsible for completing the work is to be entered onto the Sub Master. Multiple copies of Sub Masters may be required, depending on the number of persons assigned to complete the work.

8. As each piece of equipment and/or general task is completed, the employee enters his/her **initials** and the date of completion on the sub master. The completed Sub Master Weekly Schedule Sheet is returned to the Chief Engineer.

9. The Chief engineer is to review each Sub Master Sheet returned to ensure that the Preventive Maintenance has been completed.

10. The Sub Masters are to be filed in a dated binder for one year in the Chief engineer's Office. At year-end, the binders are to be put in permanent storage and kept for legal reasons.

11. If the Department has a personal computer and uses the Chief Software, all fire protection equipment of the property shall be identified under tag number series.

Subject: FIRE PROTECTION PREVENTIVE MAINTENANCE	Section: PROGRAMS

FIGURE 1. - FIRE PROTECTION MAINTENANCE SCHEDULE

EQUIPMENT	MAINTENANCE SCHEDULE
Electric Fire Pump	Tested Monthly - Inspect the condition or the pump, bearings, staffing boxes, suction pipe strainers and the various other details pertaining to the driver and control equipment.
Diesel Fire Pump	Test weekly - Run Time minimum 30 minutes
Fire Tanks	Inspected yearly including float switch
Fire Standpipe Valves	Sealed Valves - inspect weekly Locked Valves - Inspect monthly Tamper Switches - inspect and test monthly All Valves - annually valve stems should be oiled or grease. The valves shall be completely closed and reopened to test their operation and to distribute the lubricant
Fire Department connections	Inspect the following monthly: - Pump Test Header - Hose Connections - Roof Manifolds - Siamese connections
Indicator Post valves	Test quarterly
Fire Hoses	Re-racked annually
Sprinkler Heads	Visual inspection monthly. Sprinkler should be free from corrosion, foreign materials, paints and not bent or damaged.
Sprinkler Flow Indicators	Water flow indicators tested every two months
Pressure Gage (s)	Calibration Test - Every 5 years
Main Drains	Flow test quarterly as per NFPA 13 Chapter 2.6. 1
Fire Extinguishers	Inventory taken and visual inspection monthly (sign and date extinguisher tag). Maintenance yearly by specialist contractor.
Hydrants (Private)	Inspect monthly Open and close annually Perform maintenance procedure semi-annually as recommended by manufacturer
Preaction/Deluge Detection	Test semi-annually, flow test System sprinkler
Preaction/Deluge System	Test annually

Subject:		Section		
FIRE PROTECTION PREVENTIVE MAINTENANCE		PROGRAMS	Number: 2.4	

Dry/Preaction/Deluge Systems	Inspect air pressure and water pressure weekly in cold weather. inspect enclosure daily inspect priming water level quarterly.
Low-point Drains	Test in the Fall
Dry-Pipe Valves	Trip-Test annually in the Spring Full Row trip test every 3 years in the Spring
Quick Opening Devices (a.k.a. Accelerators)	Test semi annually
Antifreeze Solution	Test annually
Cold Water Valves	Close valves in the Fall Open valves in the Spring
Gravity Tanks	Inspect water level monthly In cold water, inspect heating mechanism (if applicable) daily Inspect condition of tanks bi-annually
Pressure Tanks	Inspect water level and pressure monthly In cold weather, inspect heat enclosure daily Inspect condition of tanks bi-annually
Fire Extinguishers	Complete discharge and hydrostatic tested every 12 years or sooner as required by code
Fire Alarm Stations	Visual inspection weekly
Coded Pull Boxes 1/12 of Total Fire Alarm Stations and Detection Devices	Actual pull test every 3 months of all stations 1/12 total tested monthly so all units are tested at least yearly.
Inspection OuTLine of Each Months 1/12 System Alarm Test (i.e. floors 1 through 3 tested If hotel is a 36 storey property)	A. Pull stations operated by pulling handle B. Smoke detectors tested by operating test button or magnet (test set) Heat detectors tested by removal of fusible link (test set) C. Water flow switch tested by operating inspector; test valve on floor D. Tamper switch on sprinkler system, operated by turn valve ¼ turn Main fire alarm panel annunciator proper alarm zone E. Firefighters telephone operated properly F. All fire alarm zones can be reset and confirmed free of trouble conditions. (If applicable) send alarm signals over telephone wires to the central stations or fire department to confirm operation

Subject: **FIRE PROTECTION PREVENTIVE MAINTENANCE**	Section PROGRAMS	Number: 2.4	

Escape Routes including Exit Signs	Full inspection at least monthly
Emergency Generator (s)	To be tested weekly and run for 30 minutes on load
Pre alarm Bells/ Speakers	Tested every two months (voice tested if P.A. is provided). Entire system to be tested as during full evacuation of property.
Battery Test	Once a year Operate entire bell/voice system for 3 minutes on standby power if provided.
Emergency Battery Lighting	Once every 6 months Operate emergency lighting for 1 hour on battery standby
Generator/Fire Pump Battery	Weekly Perform hydrometer float test of battery cells. Check voltage and output of battery charger.
Range Hood Fire Extinguisher System	Inspected, tested, bottle weight every 6 months
Kitchen Range Hood Filters	At least weekly **Dirty filters removed, clean filters** installed
Fire Fighting Equipment	Monthly (Documented evaluation of instructions in use and equipment)
Fire Fighting Equipment	Yesrly Actual fire fighting by fire brigade and selected employees
Chemical Fire Proofing of Continuous Service Kitchen Exhaust Ducts	Every 2 months or more often if local conditions require
Chemical Fire Proofing of Infrequently Used Kitchens	As required, at least once a year
Automatic Fire Doors	Monthly tested for heat and smoke **reaction**
Other Fire Doors	Checked every 6 months
Fire Cart/Backpack	Monthly Inventory taken
Main Gas Valve	Yearly checked by gas company for closing
Elevator Pits	Monthly rubbish removed and equipment cleaned (**not to be done by in-house employee 04**

Subject: **FIRE PROTECTION PREVENTIVE MAINTENANCE**	Section **PROGRAMS**	Number: 2.4	Page 6 of 7
Elevators	Safety inspected as required by codes or as determined by Hospitality Hotels & Resorts Safety Department.		
Boilers and Pressure Vessels	Minimum yearly safety inspections as required by codes.		
Trash and Linen Chutes	Monthly Doors to be cleared for proper closing		
Laundry Equipment and Exhaust Ducts	Daily to be checked for lint accumulation and to be cleaned.		
Fire and Emergency Procedure Updating and Training	One day after arrival of a new staff member and in 3 months intervals thereafter. Monthly intervals for telephone operators and night staff.		

NOTE:

These are minimum requirements. If local authorities require more frequent maintenance, above schedule should be changed accordingly.

| Subject: **FIRE PROTECTION PREVENTIVE MAINTENANCE** | Section **PROGRAMS** | Number: 2.4 | Page 7 of 7 |

FIGURE 2. - GENERAL TASKS

The following list provides a general overview,. It may be expanded by considering the specific requirements of a particular hotel. The time periods mentioned are for reference only and may vary greatly, depending on the type of hotel and any local regulations.

TASK	RECOMMENDED TIME PERIOD
All emergency plans should be checked, updated and coordinated with the fire department	Yearly
Emergency procedures must be tested for their effectiveness (i.e. bomb threats, evacuation drills.)	Yearly
Simulated fire alarm drills should be conducted with as much realism as possible on each shift	Monthly
Escape route identification must be checked and missing signs must be replaced, any obstructions must be removed.	2 to 6 weeks
The availability of emergency instructions (safety measures) in guest rooms, corridors, lobbies, etc. must be checked and missing items must be replaced.	1 to 6 weeks
The availability of emergency instructions in guest rooms (room cards) must be checked	Daily, with room make-up
All areas of the building must be inspected to detect any changes in fire load, accumulation of dirt or trash, etc.	1 to 6 weeks
The proper designation of non-smoking areas must be checked	2 to 8 weeks
The observation of no-smoking regulations must be checked	Continuously
Property and functional cleaning procedures, in particular the punctual emptying of waste baskets, trash cans and ashtrays, must be checked (especially after festivities during exhibitions, etc.)	As required
Kitchen areas must be checked for accumulation of combustible materials such as oil and grease, especially in hoods and ventilation ducts	1 to 4 weeks
The proper storage of grease and oil rags (i.e. approved containers)	As required

PROPERTY OPERATIONS POLICIES AND PROCEDURES

Subject:	**SAFETY TAG/LOCKOUT**	Section: PROGRAMS

PURPOSE: To prevent injury or loss of life due to the inadvertent start up of equipment, or to systems being repaired and/or installed.

POLICY: The Chief engineer will implement and strictly enforce the Safety Tag Lockout Policy.

STANDARDS:
1. Safety tags and mechanical lock-outs are to be issued to each member of the department.
2. Safety tags and mechanical lock-outs are to be affixed to equipment disconnects, valves, etc. prior to repairs and installations.
3. Safety tags and mechanical lock outs are to be removed by the originator or the Chief Engineer **ONLY**.
4. Employees are to be given a copy of this procedure and trained in its use at least annually.
5. Safety tags and mechanical lock-outs are to be used by outside contractors.

PROCEDURE
1. Safety tags and mechanical lockouts with non-identical padlocks are to issued top each member of the Engineering Department. A supply of safety tags is to be readily available within the maintenance shop area. A typical example of a safety tag, as in Figure 1, can be obtained from an electrical supply house.
2. Before commencing any work that require shutting off electrical circuit breakers, disconnects, or closing of water, steam or gas valves, and any equipment which stores energy, the Engineering Department member must attach a signed and dated safety tag and mechanical lock-out. This will prevent the inadvertent start-up of equipment or system, which could result in personal injury or loss of life.
3. After the equipment has been affixed with a safety tag and mechanical lock-out, the department member will attempt to start the equipment, in order to ensure it has been properly immobilized.
4. Extreme caution is to be exercised in order to ensure zero mechanical state has been achieved. As an example, equipment which is hydraulic or pneumatic operated may need to be de-energized.
5. If more than one department member is working on the same equipment or system, each member must attach his/her respective safety tag and mechanical lock-out.

Subject:	Section	Number: 2.6	Page 2 of 3
SAFETY TAG/LOCKOUT	PROGRAMS		

6. After the work has been completed, the safety tag and mechanical lock-out is to be removed by the originator or the Chief engineer; but, only after it has been thoroughly determined to be safe to do so. Removal by any other person is forbidden.

7. Department employees are to be given a copy of this procedure and trained in its proper use and implementation at least annually. Training documentation must be maintained on file.

8. Documented procedure training must be provided for employees, other than the Engineering Department, who are working in areas affected by equipment, i.e. laundry, kitchen.

9. This policy applies to outside contractors working within the building. It is to be monitored and enforced without exception.

10. Ensure that any new equipment, purchased or overhauled, can accommodate mechanical lock outs.

11. This policy is to be strictly adhered to.

Subject:	Section		
SAFETY TAG/LOCKOUT	PROGRAMS	Number: 2.6	Page 3 of 3

Figure 1. - SAFETY TAG EXAMPLE

DO NOT REMOVE THIS TAG

IT IS A VIOLATION OF PLANTRULES
**TO DO SO WITHOUT AUTHORITY WILL MEAN DISCIPLINARY ACTION
SEE OTHER SIDE**

PLASTIC CLIP

DO NOT OPERATE

SIGNED BY
DATE

WTAG-71 A   Thomas and Betts

PROPERTY OPERATIONS POLICIES AND PROCEDURES

Subject: INFRA-RED THERMOGRAPHIC SURVEY ~~Section: PROGRAMS~~

PURPOSE: To reduce the risk of fires and failure of electrical services and mechanical systems.

POLICY: The Chief Engineer is to conduct an annual infrared thermographic survey of all electrical distribution systems and major mechanical equipment.

PROCEDURE

1. Identify And develop a schedule of all electrical distribution boards, switchgear, electrical panels and mechanical equipment where heat can be generated or lost unnecessarily.

2. Locate the nearest suitably qualified contractor to undertake the survey. Ensure that the contractor has the most modem and appropriate thermal imagers to achieve the highest quality results.

3. Coordinate the survey with other hotels in your area to reduce costs of surveys.

4. Ensure that the data is recorded on videotape for later analysis and permanent storage of information.

5. Provide copies of survey results to Divisional Engineer.

6. Ensure that any necessary work, identified in the survey, is completed as soon as possible.

7. Advise Divisional Engineer that all work has been satisfactorily completed.

PART3

SYSTEMS

3.0 SYSTEMS

3.1	Water Treatment
3.2	Pool & Spa Treatment
3.3	Water Fountain Treatment
3.5	Key Control
3.6	L.P. Bacteria

PROPERTY OPERATIONS POLICIES AND PROCEDURES

Subject:	**WATER TREATMENT** Section: SYSTEMS	
PURPOSE:	To extend the life of piping systems and related equipment through protection against corrosion, scale build up and microbiological growth and reduce operating costs by improved efficiency.	
POLICY:	The Chief Engineer will implement and monitor the Water Treatment Policy and maintain a water treatment service contract.	
STANDARDS:	1.	The services of a Water Treatment Company will be retained.
	2.	The water treatment service company must supply required chemicals and all other services identified in the procedure.
	3.	Condenser water analysis tests will be conducted and recorded **daily** and water chemistry will be adjusted accordingly.
	4.	Boiler water, feed water and steam condensate analysis tests will be conducted and recorded daily and chemistry will be adjusted accordingly.
	5.	Close loop water system analysis tests will be conducted and recorded weekly and water chemistry will be adjusted accordingly.
PROCEDURE	1.	A service contract is to be retained from a water treatment service company.
	2.	The service company will supply the required chemicals as follows:
		Condenser Water Scale Corrosion Inhibitors - In most cases this will be of the molybdate/polymer/phosphonate type, suitable for operation in the pH range of 7.0 - 8.5 It will not contain free mineral acids or chromates. The use of **acid is** to be **avoided** unless **approved** by the Divisional Director.
		Condenser Water Microbicides - Two functionally different microbicides will be used on a rotating basis. Non-oxidizers are preferred, but bromine release chemicals are acceptables.
		Closed System Corrosion Inhibitors - A buffered boron nitride corrosion inhibitor will be used.

Subject:	Section	Number: 3.1	
WATER TREATMENT	SYSTEMS		

Boiler Oxygen Scavenger - This is a catalyzed sulfite product used to remove dissolved oxygen from the water.

Boiler Corrosion and Deposit Inhibitor - Generally this is a multi component formulation and is either a phosphate or polymer based products.

Steam and Condensate Corrosion Inhibitor - A neutralized amine based products, food grade, must be used.

3. The service company is to provide the following additional services:

A **monthly** (minimum) service visit at which time all treated systems are to be analyzed and daily/weekly chemical log sheets reviewed. A **field** service report detailing findings and **recommendations** must be prepared.

Training of operating personnel in the proper chemical test procedure and instruction on the proper handling of chemicals in terms of safety and government regulations, including Material Safety Data Sheets (MSDS) or equivalent.

Provide chemical test kit equipment and chemical log sheets for all applicable systems.

Representation each time a cooling tower, water side of a condenser, chiller or boiler is open for inspection or overhaul. A field service inspection report detailing the effectiveness of the treatment program together with any recommendations prepared.

Technical assistance for any water treatment problem upon request.

A quarterly chemical system analysis of all treated systems performed in the service company's corporate testing laboratory.

4. The Chief Engineer will ensure the following is performed:

Conduct **daily** analytical tests on the condenser water and adjust the water chemistry accordingly.

The test is to **determine** total dissolved solids, pH and chemical inhibitor levels.

Conduct **daily** analytical tests on the boiler water, feedwater and steam condensate and adjust chemistry accordingly.

The tests are to determine the following:

Subject:	Section	Number: 3.1	Page 3 of 5
WATER TREATMENT	SYSTEMS		

Total Alkalinity and Hydroxide level
Oxygen scavenger level Corrosion
Deposit inhibitor level Condensate
pH
Chloride level (feedwater and boiler water)
TDS (feedwater and boiler water)
Hardness (feedwater)

Conduct **weekly** analytical tests on the closed loop chilled water and heating hot water systems and adjust the water chemistry accordingly.

The tests is to determine the concentration of corrosion **inhibitors**.

The results of all the above tests and chemical adjustments made are to be entered in a chemical log specifically designed for the purpose. The log sheets are to be supplied by the water treatment service company.

Recommendations by the water treatment service company are to be implemented and complied with.

    q.   Copies of all reports developed by the water treatment service company are to be maintained in department files.

  s. Feeding equipment and controller specifications for the condenser water and closed loop Are as follows:

      d. The control equipment for the condenser water will be of the type characterized as meterfeed, conductivity bleed, lock out on biocide addition.

Chemical feed based on system bleed is only acceptable through the use of a conductivity controller.

Note: The Portions of this equipment are as following:

Water motor on cooling tower make-up - The Meter is to be installed in an appropriate location to prevent freezing. The meter controller is to incorporate circuitry designed to turn the chemical pump on and off for adjustable time periods in proportion to the make-up water volume.

Conductivity sensor in the bypass loop - The Controller circuitry is to open a solenoid blowdown valve when the condenser water conductivity rises to an adjustable set point. The condenser cooling water system must be designed so that uncontrolled bleed does not occur.

Subject:	Section		
WATER TREATMENT	SYSTEMS	Number: 3.1	Page 4 of 5

Seven or fourteen day timer - Circuitry within the timer is to provide outlets for two chemical pumps. The date, time of day and let length of pump iti g time are to be adjustable. The timer is to be equipped with a flip-top relay or solid state programmable circuit so that the pumps will automatically alternate throughout the timer cycle. Circuitry is to be provided to lock out the blowdown solenoid during, and for an adjustable time period follow 19. biocide addition.

Controller sensor - Provision 11 is to be made in the controller to sense when the co11 denser water pumps are not operating. This may be accomplished with the cooling tower circulating pumps usi 119 a flow sensor or with19 the controller across the pumps. During shutdown periods, no chemicals will be fedor blowdown permitted.

Control equipment - The equipment 11th may be composed of a single integrated unit or separately supplied compo11ents so long as the individual compo 11ants **integrate** smoothly. SuitabLe equipments is available from : Auto trol Corp., Mi lwauk i e. WI wisconsin Lakewood Instruments, Inc,Compton, CA Moor Control Inc. Muskogee, Oklahoma And others.

    g.   Three chemical pumps are to be installed. The pumps will be of the electronic diaphragm type. The maximum output rate is to be specified by the water treatment service company. The pumps are to be capabLe of pumping agah 1s t a h ead one and 011e-half times the anticipated pressure at the point of injection.

    i.   The chemical pumps may discharge either into the cooling tower basin or i 11 to the system p ip i ng. If injection is made into system piping, removable stainless steel injection quills (corporation stops) are to be installed.

    k.   A solenoid blowdown valve a11d thro Uling valve are to be Installed 011 the hot water return to the tower side of the co11densers.

    m.   By-pass pot feeders are to be installed across the piping of the hot water boiler feed and chilled water pumps. The pot **feeders are** to be ASME tested a11d have at least 10 liters capacity a11d have a pressure rating two times the anticipated system pressure at the point of i 1jectio11.

6.   Feeding equipment 1t for the steam boilers are as follows:

    c.   Chemical feed is to be automated, with separate feed pumps and solution tanks for each chemical formula. The pumps are to be activated in conjm1ctio11wi th the feed water pump ht order to maintain desired chemical levels in the water.

    e.   Chemicals are to be fed either into the feed water tank below the water 1'10" directly i1t1o the boiler. A stainless steel quill will be used for each chemical injection point. If fed to the feed water tanks, maximum protectio1i1s assured for pre-boiler and steam condensate lines.

Subject:	Section		
WATER TREATMENT	SYSTEMS	Number: 3.1	Page 5 of 5

7. Periodic boiler blowdown is required for control of chemical levels and elimination of contaminants.

   d. Phosphate based corrosion and deposit inhibitors precipitate contaminates out of solution. This necessitates blowdown from the bottom of the boiler.

   The frequency of blowdown is determined by testing the chloride level of the feed water. This indicates boiler water cycles of concentration.

   Automatic blowdown equipment is not to be used for bottom level boiler blowdown.

   j. Polymer based corrosion and deposit inhibitors maintain contaminates in solution.

   Slowdown is determined by TDS (Total Dissolved Solids) levels.

   Automatic surface skimmer controller may be used for surface level blowdown.

8. It Is recommended that corrosion coupons be installed in the condenser water system. This will help verify the effectiveness of the water treatment program in preventing corrosion.
Most water treatment service companies will provide this service, installation and testing.

9. Storage, handling and disposal of chemicals is subject to environmental health protective measures, including secondary containment. Ensure that chemicals stored within the same containment area are compatible with each other. Review MSDS.

10. Continuous on demand eyewash stations must be installed in the vicinity of chemical feed equipment.

11. A drum disposal plan is to be provided by the chemical service company, or a mini-porta feed system installed (disposable drums are not used).

PROPERTY OPERATIONS POLICIES AND PROCEDURES

Subject:	**POOL & SPA TREATMENT** Section: SYSTEMS
PURPOSE:	To protect against corrosion, scale build-up and microbiological growth in the mechanical systems and provide guests with safe sparkling clear water.
POLICY:	The Chief Engineer is to implement and monitor the Pool and Spa Treatment Program in accordance with industry standards, governing codes, and good operating practices.

STANDARDS:

1. **Accurate** chemical tests are to be conducted and chemicals adjusted accordingly on pools and spas.
2. The **recommended** levels of chlorine, pH, alkalinity, and hardness are to be maintained.
3. The filtration systems are to be operated and maintained in **accordance** with manufacturer's recommendations.
4. Operating log sheets are to be maintained.
5. Surfaces, decks and adjacent areas are to be thoroughly cleaned and sanitized as frequently as conditions require.
6. Environmental health protective measures are to be **maintained** for the storage and use of chemicals.

PROCEDURE

1. It is important that accurate pool an spa water chemical tests are conducted and the chemicals adjusted accordingly to ensure sparkling clean water, protection of equipment from the corrosion and scale deposits. The test are to be conducted (at a minimum) in accordance with governing codes.

2. The following is a description of the water **properties** controlled:

    FIRE CHLORINE - Free chlorine is the most effective bactericide form of chlorine. Its presence provides the immediate kill properties for destroying bacteria and algae on contact.

    TOTAL CHLORINE - Total chlorine is the measure of the Free chlorine plus the amount of chlorine in the water that has already combined with material s dissolved, or already in suspension in the water. As a bactericide it is not as effective as Free chlorine.

Subject:	Section	Number: 3.2	Page 2 of 5
POOL & SPA TREATMENT	SYSTEMS		

pH (PHENOL RED TEST) - pH factor indicates the acid or alkaline nature of the water. Sterilization of pool water is most effectively carried out in slightly alkaline conditions. Acid water is corrosive and also allows the chlorine to pass off in the form of a gas. Highly alkaline water retards the effectiveness of the chlorine that may be present. Phenol Red is the most accurate indicator.

ALKALINITY - alkalinity has a substantial effect on and in the pH of water. If the alkalinity is too low, the pH will rise and fall erratically. High alkalinity levels cause high pH values which reduces the effective the chlorine has a sanitizer.

HARDNESS - The water hardness test includes a measurement of the magnesium and calcium present. These materials, in combination with carbonate, form scale. These deposits (sometimes referred to as calcium deposits) will form at the air-water sidewall line as evaporation takes place. In the presence of high pH (greater than 8.0), these deposits will form inside piping and fittings. They will restrict water flow, the mechanical operation of flow meters, injectors, etc., and will adversely affect the operation of water heaters. In time, these deposits will cause metal surfaces to corrode beyond repair.

3. The following chemical ranges are guidelines. Local codes will dictate specific chemical ranges to be maintained.

   d. **SWIMMING POOLS**

   Free Chlorine - 0.6 - 1.0 PPM
   Total Chlorine - 1.0 - 2.0 PPM
   pH - 7.2 - 7.6 PPM
   Alkalinity - 100 - 150 PPM
   Hardness - 200-250 PPM which a pH less than 8.0

   SPAS

   Free Chlorine - 3.0 - 5.0 PPM
   Total Chlorine - as low as possible, always less than half of the free chlorine concentration.
   pH - 7.4 - 7.8
   Alkalinity - 120- 150 PPM

4. The best source of information on the operation and maintenance of the pool and spa equipment is the literature from the manufacturer.

   General requirements as follows:

   PUMP - Operate the pump enough hours each day to maintain clean water. Check and clean hair/lint basket at least daily. The pump should be capable of recirculating the entire volume in six (6) hours for pools and four (4) hours for spas.

Subject:	Section	Number: 3.2	Page 3 of 5
POOL & SPA TREATMENT	SYSTEMS		

FILTER - Backwash or clean filter periodically. Check manufacturer's manual for frequency and/or pressure gauge readings. Do not allow water discharged from filter to come in contact with lawn or shrubbery; chemicals in the water may kill plant life.

HEATER - Have the heater and controls checked by a service company, or qualified staff members, each year for proper operation.

For lighting of the pilot light and/or making adjustments, follow all directions printed inside the heater cabinet.

AUTOMATIC CHLORINATOR - Use only the type of chlorine product recommended by the manufacturer or professional distributor. Never mix different types of chemical compounds; serious injury may result. Chlorine gas is not to be used.

AUTOMATIC POOL CLEANER - Operate for the amount of time recommended by the manufacturer. Most units are designed to operate only when the filtration system is running. Clean strainers as necessary.

LADDER/HANDRAILS - Check all bolts and tighten regularly.

SKIMMER BASKETS - Check daily and clean when required to allow maximum skimming action and water circulation.

CLEANING EQUIPMENT - Plastic cleaning equipment will last longer if stored out of direct sunlight. Keep telescopic poles, brushes and leaf nets away from deck to avoid tripping over them.

WINTER COVERS./SOLAR BLANKETS - Clean prior to folding and storing to protect against odours, mildew stain and sticking.

GASKETS AND O-RINGS - Lubricate with a special lube available from dealer. Do not use petroleum-based greases.

TEST KIT - Store in a cool, dark place away from chemicals and heaters. Rinse test chambers after each use. Always use fresh reagents at the start of each season.

EQUIPMENT WINTERIZING - Where freeze conditions exist, refer to manufacturer or dealer for protection of all equipment.

Subject:	Section	Number: 3.2	
POOL & SPA TREATMENT	SYSTEMS		

5. A swimming pool and spa operating log is to be used to record water chemistry test results, backwash, water clarity, temperature and other operations. This log is important documentation which can be useful if problems arise. Refer to Figure 1 for an example swimming pool and spa log sheet which can be modified to suit your needs

6. The swimming pool and spa operating log is to be completed daily (minimum).

7. Due to the inherent design and purpose of spas, water conditions and quality are critical. The small volume of water, high water turnover rate, high temperature, water agitation and high bather load, contribute to rapid depletion of disinfectant and pH levels. Therefore, frequent testing and/or use of continuous reading device are recommended.

8. The frequency of cleaning, brushing, vacuuming and sanitizing of the equipment and deck areas should be determined based on the number of users. Heavily used facilities may have to be cleaned every 24 hours, preferably at night or during off hours. When using chemical compounds for cleaning purposes, the manufacturer's safety recommendations must be observed.

9. Storage of pool chemicals is subject to environmental health protective measures, including secondary containment and chemical compatibility a per MSDS. In most cases, a continuous on-demand eye wash station is required in the pool equipment room.

Subject:	Section		
POOL & SPA TREATMENT	SYSTEMS	Number: 3.2	Page 5 of 5

FIGURE 1. -SWIMMING POOL LOG SHEET EXAMPLE

DATE	CHLORINE		TOTAL			BACKWASH		WATER		POOL
	FREE	TOTAL	ALK	pH	HARDNESS	YES	NO	CLARITY	TEMP.	VAC.

PROPERTY OPERATIONS POLICIES AND PROCEDURES

Subject:	WATER FOUNTAIN TREATMENT	Section: SYSTEMS

PURPOSE: To protect against corrosion, scale build-up and harmful microbiological growth in outdoor and indoor fountains.

POLICY: The Chief Engineer is to implement and monitor the Fountain Treatment System in accordance with these procedures.

STANDARDS:
1. A visual inspection of the fountain (s) is to be made daily.
2. Water and filter systems are to be maintained and operated according to the manufacturer's instructions and industry standards.
3. Fountain surfaces and adjacent areas are to be cleaned as frequently as conditions require.
4. While fountains do not present the health hazards associated with swimming pools and spas, proper levels of pH and chlorine must be maintained for purposes of algae control and water clarity.

PROCEDURE
1. The water fountains are to be visually inspected daily for water clarity and condition of the mechanical equipment. It is recommended that inspections be scheduled as part of morning rounds.

2. Frequency of chemical testing is to be established based on size and location of the fountain. Outdoor systems will require more frequent testing and treatment, due to the effect of the sun, atmospheric conditions and geographical locations.

3. The following chemical ranges are to be maintained:

   Free Chlorine - 0.6 to **1.0 PPM**
   Total Chlorine - 1.0 to 2.0 **PPM**
   pH factor - 7. 2 to 7.6
   Alkalinity - 100 to 150 **PPM**
   Hardness - **200 PPM**

4. Water Fountains are to be drained, cleaned, refilled and chemically charged as frequently as operating conditions require.

5. The water fountain mechanical equipment is to be **maintained per** the manufacturer's recommendations.

6. Hard water spots on the water fountain surface s and adjacent areas are to be removed as conditions require.

7. Due to the variety of fountain designs and operating conditions, additional **procedures** may be necessary to ensure a clean and attractive setting.

PROPERTY OPERATIONS POLICIES AND PROCEDURES

Subject:	**KEY CONTROL**	Section: SYSTEMS

PURPOSE: To safeguard the integrity of the hard-key system.

POLICY: The Chief Engineer is responsible for monitoring the inventory and insurance of hard keys. Approval must be obtained from the Divisional Director of Operations for any other employees to monitor this system.

STANDARDS:

1. A secure area for storage of keys and record will be provided and a file inventory of original keys is to be maintained.

2. A key issue file system is to be established and maintained.

3. Audits of master keys are to be conducted semi annually.

4. No master key will be issued without written authorization from both the General Manager and Chief Engineer. All other keys are to be approved by the respective department head.

5. Keys are hotel property and must be returned to the Chief Engineer upon termination or employment.

PROCEDURE

1. Establish a secure area in the maintenance shop for key storage and records. A designated key room is ideal. If this is not possible, the Engineering office area will be acceptable. The key storage area is to have limited access and kept locked when not in use.

2. Purchase a key cabinet for storage of the original key file inventory. The capacity of the key cabinet should be determined by counting the individual coded keys, either from the bitting list or the finish hardware schedule. The cabinet should have the ability to be expanded by additional panels, if required. The key cabinet is to be locked when not in use.

3. **Follow manufacturer's instructions to establish the key file inventory system needed to control keys.**

4. Review the bitting list and finish hardware schedule thoroughly. Use the architectural plans as a guide to verify location and identification of keys to ensure correct match-up with locksets.

5. All duplication keys are to be identified by stamping with the corresponding alphabetical letter and numbers assigned to it by the billing identify *any* duplicated key.

6. Develop a key issue file system by department using 75mm x 125mm index cards for each department, as in Figure 1. A key issue card is to be kept on file for each key issued.

| Subject: KEY CONTROL | Section SYSTEMS | Number: 3.5 | Page 2 of 4 |

7. A semi-annual audit of all master **keys** is to be conducted by the Chief Engineer, using the fire index. The purpose of this audit is to account for all master keys and to verify that each master key is in the possession of the person issued the key. Any discrepancy found is to be noted on the respective file card and reported to the General Manager.

8. Keys will be issued to employees with written authorization via the Key Request form only, as in **Figure 2.** Master key require approval by the General Manager and Chief Engineer. All other keys issued must be approved by the respective department head.

9. An adequate supply of key blanks is to be **maintained** and kept secured.

10. All keys remain hotel properties and must be **returned** to the Chief Engineer upon employment termination. It is the responsibility of the employee and the Personnel Department to ensure that the key is accounted for and acknowledge by a receipt from the Chief Engineer.

11. If the department has a personal computer or access to one, the key issue file system can be computerized, eliminating the need for the manual index cards.

Subject:	Section	Number: 3.5	Page 3 of 4
KEY CONTROL	SYSTEMS		

Figure . - KEY ISSUES FILE CARD EXAMPLE

Name: _____ Key #:

Department: --

Signature: -

Date Issued: _____

Date Added in the d: -

Date Returned: _____

Where key will be kept:

:_ _ _ _ _ _ _ _ _ _ _ s _

What Keys fits:------------------------------------

Subject:	Section	Number: 3.5	Page 4 of 4
KEY CONTROL	SYSTEMS		

Figure 2. KEY REQUEST FORM

Hospitality HOTELS & RESORTS   KEY REQUEST

Date

Requiert
Department Ke

Requested Reason for

Request

RbUOiRbb
APPROVALS|QNAI☐Rb§

_____ Chief Engineer

Department Head

I, The undersigned receiver of above requested key, understand that loss of such key must be reported immediately to the Chief Engineer, and to my department head. Further understand I must return such key to the Chief Engineer upon my termination or upon request of the Chief Engineer.

Key   No.   Received   on

By

PROPERTY OPERATIONS POLICIES AND PROCEDURES

Subject: LEGIONELLA PNEUMOPHILA BACTERIA ~~Section: SYSTEMS~~

PURPOSE: To reduce the risk of contamination of air and water systems.

POLICY: The Chief Engineer will have tests conducted for the presence of Legionella Pneumophila bacteria on all exposed water system, such as cooling towers, domestic hot water systems, whirlpools/spas, QUARTERLY.

PROCEDURE

1. Identify A suitably qualified laboratory able to conduct tests for Legionella bacteria.
2. Obtain sterilized sampling bottles for dispatching samples of treated water system via courier to the testing laboratory.
3. **Obtain and file test results for future reference.**
4. Take the necessary action to sterilize any treated system where Legionella is detected and submit samples for further testing.
5. Forward copy of test results top Divisional Engineer.

PART4

GENERAL

4.0 GENERAL

4.1	Tools & Equipment
4.2	Building Documents
	Service Contracts
	Department Rules
4.4	Air Conditioning Standards
	Basics of Psychrometrics
4.5	Additional standards
4.6	
4.7	
4.8	

PROPERTY OPERATIONS POLICIES AND PROCEDURES

Subject:	**TOOLS & EQUIPMENT** Section: GENERAL
PURPOSE:	To standardize and control the Engineering Department tools and equipment.
POLICY:	The Chief Engineer is to purchase the recommended tools and equipment ensure that they are distributed, maintained and inventoried.

STANDARDS:

1. The recommended tools and equipment list will be used as a guideline for the purchase of tools.
2. The required hand tool list **will** be maintained and carried by each maintenance person.
3. Tools and equipment are to be **commercial grade,** have hotel identification markings and be maintained in good working condition.
4. Tools and equipment are to be inventoried, stored and controlled as detailed in the procedure.

PROCEDURE

1. The tool and equipment list, as in **Figure 1,** is to be used as a guideline only to establish the type of tools and equipment required. Additional tools may be required or some of the tools not required; depending on the number of employees, their skill level and type of hotel. Quantities will be determined by the size of the hotel, number of employees and their skill level.
2. Each department member is to provide, or be provided with, the required personal hand tools as listed in **Figure 2.** The decision to provide the tools or have each member purchase their own is to be determined by each hotel.
3. A list of personal hand tools provided is to be maintained on file and each department member is to sign for all tools received.
4. Each member of the Engineering Department **is to carry** his/her personal hand tools (excluding trades such as painters) in a tool pouch during working hours.
5. Each department member is **responsible** for replacement of any personal hand tool that is lost or damaged due to misuse or neglect.
6. Personal hand tools are to be **replaced by the hotel** f they are damaged or broken in the normal course of work. This will be determined by the Chief Engineer.

Subject:	Section		
TOOLS AND EQUIPMENT	GENERAL	Number: 4.1	Page 2 of 9

7. All tools and equipment to be commercial grade, have hotel identification markings and are to be maintained in good working order. This also applies to hand tools where department members are required to provide their own. It is recommended that each hand tool be marked with the individual's initial.

8. **A complete list** of the Engineering Department tools and equipment is to be maintained in departmental files. **A semi-annual tool and equipment inventory**, including personal hand tools, is to be conducted by the Chief Engineer.

9. **N** order to prevent theft, both tools and equipment and personal hand tools are to be stored in **a secure area** when not in use.

10. **No tool** will be removed from the property without **written authorization** from the Chief Engineer.

11. The Engineering Department tools will be used by department members **only. They are** not to be loaned to other hotel employees.

12. **All** hand tools purchased by the hotel and issued to Department personnel are to be **returned** upon termination of employment.

Subject:	Section	Number: 4.1	Page 3 of 9
TOOLS AND EQUIPMENT	GENERAL		

FIGURE 1. - TOOLS AND EQUIPMENT GUIDELINE

MECHANICAL TOOLS AND EQUIPMENT

Hand Operated oil pump Grease guns
Oil cans
Arc Welder 11g Machine, 225 amp.
Protective welding screens
Welding and cutting 119 outfit (Pona-Weld)
    Torch assembly: hose, sparker, cylinder, oxy-acetylene, cutting, tip, regulator, welding tip
Welding goggles
Arc welding helmet and goggles Safety shields
Disposable dust masks Work gloves
150 mm plastic funnels
8 m extension ladder 5 m extension ladder
2. 5m aluminum step ladder
2. Aluminum step ladder 1. 2 aluminum step ladder
High-pressure washer, 1 ½ HP motor, 220 volts, maximum pressure - 50 bars at 10ℓ/min Heavy duty wet dry vacuum, 100 tank with dolly, suction hose and heads
Portable air compressor, ¾ HP motor, 8 bars, 10m air hose with quick **release nozzle** Set of ex out bearing puller 1lg each e11t
Combination 11 3-pro 119 bear i119 puller
Set packing pullers Screw jacks
2 ton hydraulic service jack 1 ton chain lever pullers
1 ½ 1011 chain hoist (manual)
Portable circulating pump
200L stand-up drum truck 200L drum stand with handles Drill press, ¾ chuck
Be11ch grinder with wire wheels (heavy duty)
190 mm mecha 11 vise
Tap and die set (3 - 18 mm)
7 drawer rolling tool cabinet with key lock
Alignment mirrors, telescopic arm Recta1, gular inspection mag11i for Magnehelic gauge dial
Handheld velometer
Orbital sa11drewith assorted grade disks/bn.Jshes
Screw extractor and drill set
Multi-purpose utility shears (scissors) Oily waste cans, yellow
Pair PVC coated shoulders length gloves

Subject:	Section	Number: 4.1	
TOOLS AND EQUIPMENT	GENERAL		

Pair each - small, medium, large and extra large seamless PVC gloves, elbow length, chemical resistant
½" square driver socket sets: 37 pieces 3/8 square drive socket sets: 25 pieces
¼" square driver socket sets: 16 pieces
150 mm adjustable wrench (insulated handle) 250 mm adjustable wrench (insulated handle)
455 mm adjustable wrench (insulated handle)
Sets open end box combination wrench 8 - 30 mm (Service and Maintenance) 150 mm Rat Tail file with handle
Trouble light, 20 m, 3 wire with ground plug, side and switch out
150 mm vise grip
Center punch set general purpose punch set
General punch staple guns Boxes staples
Maintenance leather tool pouches with belts
Square point with turned step shovels Round point with turned step shovels 250
mm wire brushes (long handles) 420 mm hacksaws (heavy duty)
300mm hacksaw blades
Tite spot hacksaw Adjustable handle hacksaw Heavy duty hollow punch
set **Knockout** patchset
Vernier caliper with dial
Single panel welding curtain Letter size clipboard
Legal size clipboard
Wheelbarrow
Medium duty wood deck platform truck
Steel hand trucks
Steel drum dolly with 4 wheels Flammable liquid safety can
Combination 11 slip joint pliers, 65 mm , insulated Channel Lock pliers, 265 mm, insulated
Pair chemical **resistant** 11t knee high rubber boots
Pair knee high rubber boots
Click stop adjustable torque wrench
Standard steel storage cabinets with locks 90 x 45 x 180 cm
Hercules steel storage cabinets with locks, 60 x 40 x 90 cm

ELECTRICAL TOOLS AND EQUIPMENT

Non conducting step ladder
Voltage tester
Simpson variable volt/ohm meter, 5000 volts
Amprobe, 1000 amps
Fuse pullers, assorted sizes
Switch box lock out
Single keyed padlocks

Subject:	Section	Number: 4.1	Page 5 of 9
TOOLS AND EQUIPMENT	GENERAL		

Electronic solder gun and solder Pair
rubber lined lineman gloves Long nose
pliers (insulated handles)
125mm needle nose pliers (insulated handles)
150 mm side cutting pliers (insulated handles)
Electrician pliers 10" (insulated handles)
300 mm blade screwdriver
250 mm blade screwdriver
150mm blade screwdriver
150 mm phillips screwdriver
125 mm phillips screwdriver
Electric wire splicing knife
Sets robertson head screwdriver (black, green, red, yellow)
Sets nut driver (graduated sizes 3-13 mm)
Sets alien wrench (graduated sizes 1-17 mm)
Light meter
Set conduit bender
10 m u-ground extension cords
Electric lamp tester
Flashlights (waterproof)
Insulated solderless terminal kit with
Crimper/ cutter
Completely made up temporary power distribution
Panel 50 amps, plug 3 m lead to panel with 20
Amp circuit breakers and duplex plugs
Wire pull spring

PLUMBING TOOLS AND EQUIPMENT

150 mm pipe wrench
350mm pipe wrench
700 mm pipe wrench
250 mm offset hex jaw pipe wrench
300 mm (10 - 50 mm) strap wrench
Heavy duty chain wrench
Faucet wrench
Basin wrench
Toilet augers
Toilet plungers heavy duty
Heavy duty pipe vise, 150 mm
Tripod for vise
Pipe cutter
Pipe reamer
Power drain snake 20 mm x 20 m
Pipe clamps, assorted sizes

REFRIGERATION TOOLS AND EQUIPMENT

Halide leak detector
Dial-a-charge (freon)

Subject:	Section	Number: 4.1	Page 6 of 9
TOOLS AND EQUIPMENT	GENERAL		

Vacuum analyzer
Manifold
Vacuum pump
Refrigeration 1 Charger with gauges a11dhoses
¼"adaptors with gasket (used from cylinder to manifold)
Vacuum cleaner with blower (portable)
Electronic digital thermometer
Tube flaring a11d cu tti11g kit
Propane fired soldering kit with self-igniting torch
Amprobe a11d voltage tester

CARPENTRY SHOP TOOLS AND EQUIPMENT

Table saw with assorted 250 mm blades Radial arm] saw with assorted 10" blades Drill press, chuck and vise
Drill stand
125 mm shop vise
10 mm roto hammer drill with assorted bit 15mm rotary hammer drill with assorted bits Jigsaw
Belt sander with assorted grade belts
Ram set concrete anchor gu11 Circular Saw With Assorted blades (portable) Saber saw scroll
Router with assorted bits
Rubber Mallets
5 kg sledge hammer 4.5 kg ballpe11 hammer
3.5 kg ball peen hammer Claw hammer
600 mm crow bars
Clawbars
25m tape measure 10m tape measure Cold chisel
Cape chisel
Diamo11d Chisel
Set wood chisel: assorted sizes Carpenter's level (wood) Aluminum levels
Torpedo levels; alumi11um
24" bolt cutter
14" bolt cutter
Heavy duty metal & wire shearing kit
Compound action pipe a11d duct snips Pop rivet gun with assorted rivets
85 mm c-clamps
115 mm c-clamps
180 mm c-clamps
H wood clamps

136

Subject:	Section	Number: 4.1
TOOLS AND EQUIPMENT	GENERAL	

Electric hot glue gun and 100 glue sticks Variable speed
Cordless drills and charger
Electric miter box
Sets drill bits for metal (3 x 17 mm) Sets drill bits for wood (5- 20 mm) Sharpening stones
Hatchet Hand ripsaw
Hand Finish saw **Keyhole** saw
Coping saws, 2 packs blades Wood vise
Expandable wood bits
Combination square
250 mm wood rasp: fine
250 mm wood rasp: coarse Carpenter's rule
Glass cutter
Nails sets (3 sizes)
Workmates be11ch (black & decker type) Concrete drill bit set, 3 - 14 mm Eco 11 Omy carpenter tool apron 1
Utility Knives with blades
Heavy duty pencil grip etcher, electric
Utility caulk 11g guns
Case 100% silico 11e rubber sealant
Case fast seal tub and tile caulk **Number Punch** set
Lock picking kit
High security padlock : separate keys
3/4 - - 2 x 1 5/8 high security padlock, alike keys Hot galvanized 10119 link steel chain

PAINTERS TOOLS AND EQUIPMENT

Air1ess pah1t sprayer
Paint brushes 50mm 100 mm 125 mm
200 mm roller & cover Roller pans
Roller extensions
Putty knives 50 mm, 100 mm, 125 mm
Drop clothes
Disposable dust masks Seam roller
Razor knife Wallpaper smoother
Square
Paper masking machine Sanding pole
1.5 m ladder

Subject: **TOOLS AND EQUIPMENT**	Section GENERAL	Number: 4.1	Page 8 of 9

THE HOTEL SOURCE EQUIPMENT

Key cutting machine: dominion # 150 AM-MKII from Unican, North Carolina (919) 446-3321
Standard Hospitality Hotels & Resorts Hospitality cart
Standard Hospitality Hotel & Resorts fire cart
Standard Hospitality Hotels & Resorts fire suitcase
60 gallon ul listed flammable storage cabinet
Walkie Talkies

Subject:	Section	Number: 4.1	
TOOLS AND EQUIPMENT	GENERAL		

FIGURE 2. - PERSONAL HAND TOOLS

Tool pouch
Tool pouch belt
Work gloves
Flashlights
Pocket thermometer
Utility knife (retractable)
Torpedo Level
125 mm slip joint
125 mm needle nose
250mm channel lock
150mm side cutters
250 mm adjustable wrench
Volt - circuit tester
4 way screwdriver
Hex Wrench set
Sm 1ape
125 mm vise grips
Lockout & padlock

PROPERTY OPERATIONS POLICIES AND PROCEDURES

Subject:	**BUILDING DOCUMENTS**	Section: GENERAL
PURPOSE:		To ensure protection and control of the building design documents.
POLICY:		The Engineering Department will retain and safeguard copies of the building documents.
STANDARDS:	1.	A minimum of two (2) sets of as-built blueprints, two (2) sets of equipment manuals, and one (1) set of construction contract documents are to be maintained.
	2.	Only reproduced copies of building documents will be removed from the property. A log must be maintained for tracking the issuance of the documents.
	3.	As-built blueprints will **be kept current.**
	4.	Equipment warranties will be submitted to manufacturers.
PROCEDURE	1.	One (1) set of as-built blueprints must be maintained in a **secure** location, to be determined by the General Manager and the Chief Engineer. These blueprints are to be treated as legal documents with precautions taken to prevent damage from fire, water or theft.
	2.	A second working set as-built blueprints is to be stored in the maintenance shop in a steel sectional file of adequate size to permit flat storage.
	3.	One (1) set of equipment manuals is to be maintained in the Chief Engineer's office or other secure location. This set will be identified as the master set and must not leave the office, except for duplication.
	4.	A second working set of equipment manuals is to be maintained in the maintenance shop.
	5.	One (1) set of construction contract documents, consisting of the general contracT special conditions, contract plans and specifications, addendum clarifications, change orders and related revisions, and a list of all subcontractors, identified by trade, is to be maintained in the Chief Engineer's office, or other secure location.

Subject:	Section	Number: 4.2	Page 2 of 3
BUILDING DOCUMENTS	GENERAL		

6. Only reproduced copies of blueprints or equipment manuals may be removed from the property. **Permission must** be obtained from the Chief Engineers.

7. **A log** is to be maintained for any reproduced building document removed from the property. The log will include the name of person/company, reason for removal, date removed and data returned, as in **Figure 1.**

8. A **record** of all building document transmittals, from an architect, engineer or contractor, will be maintained in the department files.

9. Blueprints are to be kept current. Modifications to mechanical, plumbing or electrical systems are to be incorporated into the working set of as built.

10. Ensure that warranties for new equipment are completed and submitted to the manufacturer. A copy of all equipment warranties are to be maintained in department files.

| Subject: BUILDING DOCUMENTS | Section: GENERAL | Number: 4.2 | |

FIGURE 1. - BUILDING DOCUMENT REQUEST LOG

PERSON/ COMPANY	REASON	DATE REMOVED	DATE RETURNED

PROPERTY OPERATIONS POLICIES AND PROCEDURES

Subject:	SERVICE CONTRACTORS	Section: GENERAL
PURPOSE:	To establish guidelines and specific **recommendations** for contracting outside services.	
POLICY:	Service Contracts may be obtained for work that is beyond the scope of knowledge, skill or staffing level of the Engineering Department.	
STANDARDS :	1. The list of equipment, systems and services is to be used only as a guideline when determining which contracts may be required.	
	2. Service contracts to be obtained based on the **recommendations specifically** outlined.	
	3. Service contacts are to be periodically **analyzed** to ensure conformance to the agreement and will be evaluated annually.	
	4. The Chief Engineer is to be involved in negotiation and renewal of **all** contracts expensed to the Engineering Department.	
PROCEDURE	1. The accompanying list of equipment, systems and services is intended to be used as a guideline to determine what requires contracted labour. The majority of items should be contracted, others must be evaluated based on specific needs, such as the number of employees and skill requirements may vary depending on design, geographical location or local codes.	
	2. Service contracts may be obtained for the following equipment, systems, or services and are to be expensed to Engineering Department.	
	Elevators Chillers HVAC control s Televisions Hazardous waste removal Waste removal Pest Control Water treatment Exterior signs Point of sale system Property management system Kitchen exhaust duct cleaning/fireproofing Laundry exhaust duct cleaning Fire alarm detection system Diesel generator/fire pump	

Subject:	Section	Number: 4.4	
SERVICE CONTRACTS	**GENERAL**		

3. Equipment service contracts are to include preventive maintenance, parts, labour and emergency call-backs (if deemed necessary)., exclusive of overtime and travel time. Service contracts which charge additional costs for parts and labour for repairs discovered during scheduled inspections should be **avoided**.

4. Extended service dates (exceeding 3 years), for any service contract, should be scrutinized closely and in most cases **avoided**.

5. Annual cost adjustment for service contracts which exceed one year, if applicable, should be based on reasonable price index, such as the **Product Commodity Prices for Metals and Metal Products.**

6. Non-performance or poor workmanship **must be** included as part of the contract termination clause. A written cancellation notice, 90 days prior to the contract anniversary date, **must also be** included.

7. The three bid process **must be** used to obtain competitive pricing for service contracts. The low bid does not necessarily have to be accepted as long as the selection can be rationalized.

8. The Chief Engineer must be involved in negotiation and renewal of all service contracts expensed to the Engineering Department.

9. Each contract is to be analyzed periodically to ensure conformance to the agreement.

10. Invoices for each service contract **must be** obtained and approved for payment by the Chief Engineer.

11. A **Work Order Contract** form must be used for all service contracts.

12. Each contract is to be reviewed **annually** for competitive price, continued need and necessary modifications.

13. A copy of **all** Engineering Department service contracts is to be maintained in the department files and considered a permanent record.

14. A record of all service contracts issued is to be maintained and updated as required, as in **Figure 1.**

Subject: SERVICE CONTRACTS	Section GENERAL	Number: 4.4	Page 3 of 3

FIGURE 1. - SERVICE CONTRACT RECORD EXAMPLE

SERVICE CONTRACTS ISSUED

COMPANY NAME	DATE OF ISSUE	EXP.DATE	ANNUAL COST	TYPE OF SERVICE

PROPERTY OPERATIONS POLICIES AND PROCEDURES

Subject:	DEPARTMENT RULES Section: GENERAL
PURPOSE:	To establish and maintain Department rules designed to a chi have a high level of job performance and safety from all Property Operations personnel.
POLICY:	The Chief engineer is to develop and enforce Department Rules in addition to and consistent with all existing Hotel Rules.
STANDARDS:	1. All Department rules are to be enforce.
	2. Departmental rules will be expanded to include any individual hotel requirements.
	3. All rules will be distributed to and reviewed with each member of the engineering Department.
	4. Each member of the Department will be required to sign a statement indicating that he/she has received and understands the Department Rules.
PROCEDURE	1. The following rules will be followed by all members of the Department and enforced by the Chief Engineer:
	The **SGR program** is an integral part of the Engineering Departmental philosophy and all members of the Department will conduct themselves accordingly.
	Each member of the Department will maintain the highest standards of personal hygiene and grooming.
	An approved, clean uniform will be worn while on duty.
	Approved, clean coveralls will be worn to protect uniforms when necessary, but avoided in guest contact areas.
	Name tags must be worn at all times while on duty.
	Baseball caps are considered inappropriate and will not be worn while on duty unless it is an approved cap worn by the Roads, Walks and Ground Department.
	Appropriate, publishable footwear will be worn at all times while on duty. Steel-toed shoes/boots are recommended. Sneakers or sandals are not permitted.

Subject:	Section	Number: 4.5
DEPARTMENT RULES	GENERAL	

Only hotel authorized emblems, buttons, etc. will be worn during working hours.

Department members are expected to report for work on time. Irregular attendance or tardiness will not be tolerated.

Time card procedures must be followed exactly as prescribed. Punching in or out for another employee will not be tolerated.

The use of drugs or alcohol while on duty, or reporting for work under the influence of same, will not be tolerated and is grounds for immediate termination.

Smoking is permitted in designated areas only. Chewing of tobacco or gum while on duty is prohibited.

Except for the Hospitality mechanic, members of the Department will never enter an occupied guest room without valid and properly issued work ticket, or when dispatched to a guest room at the guest's request, via inhouse communications.

Practicing safe working habits and maintaining a safe work environment is the responsibility of each and every member of the Engineering Department.

A full complement of hand tools will be carried at all times while on duty.

Hospitality Hotels & Resorts **Safety** Tag/**Lockout** system will be observed at all times **without exception.**

A work ticket will be completed for each job assignment. Attention will be paid to filling out work tickets completely, including an accurate assessment of time spent.

All shop tools will be returned to their proper location in a clean, and workable condition.

Each member of the Department will ensure that all work areas are clean at the end of their shift.

2. The Department will be **expanded** to include any individual hotel policies, code requirements, union stipulations, etc.

Subject:	Section		
DEPARTMENT RULES	GENERAL	Number: 4.5	Page 3 of 4

3. The Chief Engineer will review the Department rules with each member of the Department.

4. After a complete review of the rules, each employee will sign a statement attesting to their knowledge and understanding of the Department Rules. The signed statement is to be kept in the employee file. See Figure 1 for an example of a Department Rule Statement.

5. Failure of any member of the Department to follow the Department rules can result in disciplinary action, suspension or termination of employment.

6. Due to the sensitivity of disciplinary measures and regulations governing the termination of an employee, it is recommended that the hotel Director of Human Resources review and approve all Department Rules.

Subject:	Section	Number: 4.5	Page 4 of 4
DEPARTMENT RULES	GENERAL		

FIGURE 1. - EMPLOYEE DEPARTMENT RULE **STATEMENT** EXAMPLE

I have reviewed all Departmental rules with the Chief Engineer, I fully Understand the rules and will comply with them.

I understand that violation of the Departmental Rules could result in disciplinary action, suspension and/or termination of employment.

_____ _____
EMPLOYEE SIGNATURE   **DATE**

PROPERTY OPERATIONS POLICIES AND PROCEDURES

Subject:	**AIR CONDITIONING**	Section: GENERAL

PURPOSE: To ensure that every hotel maintains environmental conditions within a range of comfort, whilst minimizing the costs of providing them.

POLICY: The Chief Engineer will ensure that all air conditioned spaces in public and back of house areas are maintained within a fixed range of temperature and relative humidity at the following values:

PROCEDURE

1. All associated controls will be accurately calibrated and tested on an annual basis. This must be

...	Temperature. ·	.H	
Suml l'Heure, to prohibi	a jljuS1 1!1. 8Y	tt¢6 i d §(jl ff,i, r guest,	for guest rooms, will be made
)"/intjl. guest room th room attendant.	un a r l,5'/ns J, l:l, just	d4 l'H>e • tl oint value	ach day (if necessary) by the

4. Space temperatures and relative humidity (R.H.) will be measured and recorded each day in all major public areas, e.g. lobby, restaurants and function rooms. Accurate and reliable heavy duty measuring instruments, with a resolution of 0.1 °C, will be purchased.

5. Ventilation rates, or number of air charges per hour, will be strictly observed, as per design specifications (Good practice in the industry today accepts a median value of a 10 minute air change, eg. Six times per hour). The air balance of each space will be verified each year to ensure that it is in accordance with the original design criteria.

6. Operating time schedule will be established for all conditioned and ventilated spaces, and controlled automatically, either by a computerized program or time clock. It is imperative that A.U.H. s are started early enough to allow design conditions to be reached within the space.

Subject:	Section	Number: 4.6	Page 2 of 3
AIR CONDITIONING	GENERAL		

7. All A.H.U.s. and associated equipment will be properly maintained as per manufacturer's recommendations, to ensure optimum performance at all times.

8. The Chief Engineer will prepare a written policy and instructions to all management on the establishment of a fixed range of conditions of temperature and R.H. that will be maintained within the hotel. (See Sample)

RATIONALE Air conditioning is defined as the simultaneously control of temperature, humidity, air movement and the quality of air in a space. The aggregate effect of these factors has been combined into a concept called the "Comfort Zone", under which the majority of people will feel comfortable. Comfort can be defined as any condition that when changed, will make a person uncomfortable.

A guest's opinion of a hotel is extremely dependent on the condition of the thermal environment. If he is comfortable, then he enjoys the attractions and amenities of the hotel. However, if he feels uncomfortable, then he usually focuses on the negative sensations and does not notice the positive attributes of the hotel.

Comfort conditions are based upon people being normally clothed for indoor living; engaged in only light activities such as reading, office work or occasional walking about the room; with an air velocity of 4.5 - 7.5 meters per minute; and with no radiation effects.

Relative humidity is often more difficult to control than dry-bulb (D.B.) temperature. Therefore, it must be remembered that as R.H. increases, temperature can be decreased and conversely as R.H. decreases, **temperature can be increased**. As a general guide, for every 10% change in R.H. the temperature can be adjusted by 0.5°C. R.H. above 70% and below 30% will not provide comfort conditions, regardless of the D.B. temperature.

Frequently, after determining what is desirable, it has to be determined what is possible, and then by compromise, bring the two as close together as possible.

Subject:	Section	Number: 4.6	Page 3 of 3
AIR CONDITIONING	GENERAL		

SAMPLE
MEMORANDUM

To: All Department Heads & Supervisors

From: Chief Engineer

Date:

Subject: **AIR-CONDITIONING**

The thermal conditions within all public and back of house areas in this hotel will be maintained between 21°C - 23° C during winter and 23°C - 24°C During summer at 45%/55% relative humidity.

Under no circumstances will these parameters be changed at the whim of any staff member, or to satisfy as single guest's complaint. These conditions are designed to satisfy the majority of people at all times.

All occupied spaces are monitored for compliance with the above conditions on a continuous basis, but if you are continually feeling uncomfortable, please seek technical assistance.

Part - 5

Additional standards

5 Additional standards

5.1	Third party testing of critical equipment
5.2	Engineering contract
5.3	Contract workers on premises
5.4	Shower head maintenance
5.5	Pulsating Shower head
5.6	Lint cleaning standards
5.7	Fire alarm emergency procedure
5.8	Infrared survey
5.9	Kitchen extract duct/ duct cleaning

Subject	THIRD PARTY TESTING OF CRITICAL PLANT ROOM EQUIPMENT/MACHINERIES	
Policy Number: ENG 001 Effective Date:	Superseding Policy: Page _1_ of	1
Approved by: Title		
Objective:	It is Hospitality Hotels and Resorts policy that routine preventive maintenance is carried out on all M & E equipment. However, it is the divisional policy that third party testing/certification is carried out on a regular basis on critical plant room equipment/machineries.	
Deviation: Requires written approval from the RVP		

Procedure:

C.   List of Critical Equipment / machineries

    i. Elevators Annual Certification
    ii. Boilers   Annual Certification
    iii. Pressure vessels : Annual Certification
    iv. Thermographic   : Annual Certification
    v. Duct Condition   : Every Three years Certification
    vi. Building Structural : Every Five years Certification

B.   Director of Engineering must maintain documented records of all critical equipment/ machineries including date of spare part replacement and preventive maintenance date, etc.

C.   Not less than every twelve (12) months or as indicated above, a qualified survey firm is invited to test and certify that said critical equipment/machineries is serviced and operational suitable.

D.   The cost of such test and certification is a hotel property maintenance expense, which should be projected, in the hotel's annual operating plan.

E.   Name of firm: Lloyds or a reputable local certified firm.

5.2

STANDARDS		
Subject	**ENGINEERING CONTRACT**	
Policy Number: ENG 002 Effective Date:	Superseding Policy: Page _1_ of	1
Approved by: Title		
Objective:	It is a divisional policy that any third party engagement for Engineering Projects/Works at the hotel premises is confirmed by a written work order contract, which in general is more elaborate than a standard purchase order.	
Deviation: Requires written approval from the RVP		

Procedure: (Contract document)

The Work Order Contract is a legal document stipulating the contractual obligations between the hotel and the contractor, which should include not less than the following clause:

vi. Parties, date and other general information.
vii. Full description of the scope of work, materials and labour
viii. Obligation Of hotel and third party
ix. Completion Date and delay penalties.
x. Insurance coverage, Hold Harmless Clause and Security aspects.
xi. Payment schedule and retention value.

Subject	**CONTRACTORS WORK ON PREMISES**

Policy Number: ENG 003		Page _1_ of _4_
Effective	Superseding Policy:	-
Approved by: Title		
Objective:	It is a divisional policy that any third party conducting work at the hotel is supervised by the hotel Engineering and Security Departments.	
Deviation: Requires written approval from the RVP		

Responsibilities of General Manager

Prior to the arrival on site of any contractors to carry out any work within the hotel or its grounds, they should:

5. Inform all relevant hotel staff that works are to commence, and as to the location and nature of such works, and to have regard to such works in the carrying out of their duties during the period of such works.
6. Ensure that all necessary steps are taken to inform guests, whether resident or otherwise, of the presence of the works. In the appropriate cases they should ensure that notices are provided in appropriate locations indicating the carrying out of the works.

Responsibilities of Director of Engineering

It is the responsibility of the Director of Engineering to take all necessary steps to arrange for the orderly admission to the hotel site of contractors to carry out their operations and to inform them all procedures within the hotel relevant to the carrying out their work.

He should:-

1. Advise the contractor of the hotels emergency procedures including the indication of the fire assembly points and evacuation procedures.

CONTRACTOR WORK ON PREMISES 5.3

4. Aidve   t general use of the area within the works are taking place and of the presence of movements of any large groups of people present in the hotel during the carrying of the work.
5. Ensure that the contractor complies with his obligations in connection with screening of the work from the other users of the hotel.
6. Ensure that the contractor removes any debris and waste materials from the site and that in the absence of workmen from the works that they are left in a protected, tidy and safe condition.
7. Make the contractor aware of the presence of any water, gas or electricity services, machinery, pipes, wires and cables in the vicinity of the works and of any particular dangers which they may pose in the carrying out of the work.
8. Ensure that any incident on the site involving anybody other that the workmen themselves is reported to the appropriate authorities. In the event of accidents, to the workmen on site of which the management is aware, to request the contractor to make the appropriate report in relation to this.

I. **Procedure: (General)**
J. A contract must be in placed authorizing work/project stipulating all aspects (see Engineering Contract policy)
K. A written document with workers name side of work, etc. is issued to the Security Department so that temporary name badges and time card are made and issued.

II. **Procedure: (Hot Work)**
The following procedures will be adhered to regarding issuance of Hot Work Permit.

N. **Issuing of Permits**
15. Permits for cutting, welding, brazing, pipe, sweating and the like procedures, shall be issued by the Director of Engineering or designate.
16. Permits shall be valid only for the date of which they are issued.

8. **Responsibility of Permit Issuing Department**

A preliminary inspection of the area where the work will be conducted shall be performed by the responsible authority to determine what safety precautions will be required prior to issuing the permit.

Inspect the operation site immediately prior to the operation to ensure that all of the following are complied with:

CONTRACTOR WORK   5.3

a. If possible, move the object being worked on to a location where there are no combustible (outside the building if possible). If the object cannot be moved, remove all combustible within a 10 meter radius, where a 10 meter radius clear area is not possible, clear as much as possible and cover remaining combustibles with fire resistant covers or shield with metal fire proof guards/curtains. Edges of covers at the floor shall be tight to prevent the passage of sparks underneath.

b. Cover walls or floor openings to prevent the passage of sparks.

c. Cover or shut down ducts that might carry sparks to combustibles.

d. Where open flame work is taking place, sprinkler and detection systems shall be fully operational (unless the work is being conducted on either of these systems). Where the systems are impaired, security checks must be conducted on a regular basis.

e. Show the person doing the work where the fire hose is located and verify that they and the person on fire watch know-how to operate the fire hose.

f. Show the person doing the work and the person on fire watch where the nearest fire alarm station (manual pull) is located. Verify the type know how to activate the alarm.

g. Verify that the person doing the fire watch is equipped with a fully charged minimum 5KG, ABC extinguisher.

C. **Contractor Responsibility**
12. Must obtain a permit before starting any open flame work.
13. Must provide a minimum 5 kg, fully charged ABC extinguisher.
14. Must provide a means for shielding combustibles from parks when necessary.
15. Must provide a person in addition to the performing the work for fire watch.
16. Contractor must stop work if the original conditions in the area where the work is being done, changed.
17. Must verify that equipment for open flame work is in satisfactory operating conditions.
18. Must either post the permit in the area where the work is being done or be able to produce it on demand.

D. **Responsibility of the Fire Watcher**
20. Must know how to use a portable fire extinguisher.
21. Must know the locations of the fire alarm station and the fire hose.
22. Verifies that the work area is clear of all combustibles, so that they are adequately protected.
23. Maintains a steady and uninterrupted watch to ensure that any fires are detected early on.

5. Continues the fire watch for at least a half hour after completion of the work to ensure the detection of any smoldering fires.

D. **Suspension of Work**
1. A security officer is to conduct spot checks of every permitted open flame work site.
2. Where operations are not in compliance with the above requirements, the security officer staff immediately stop the work.
3. The fire watcher is to stay at the site for at least half an hour after the work has been stopped.
4. The security officer may allow the work to resume if he/she determines that all safeguards have been put in place.

5.4

Subject	SHOWER HEAD MAINTENANCE	
Policy Number: Effective Date:	ENG 00	Superseding Policy
Approved By: Title:		
Objective:	To provide guests with clean and hygienic showerheads with optimum pressure and variable flows as per design specification.	
Procedures:		

- Open and descale the show the ads minimum two times a year, apart from Hospitality It program.
- Descaling should be carried out using chemicals recommended by the suppliers e.g. Grohclean is ideal for all GROHE fittings.
- Adequate stock of spare parts should be maintained i.e. Repair KiVO-rings, gaskets, nozzles etc.
- Recommended tools by the manufacturers should be available with the plumbers.

Deviation:
Requires written approval from the RVP

5.5

Subject	PULSATING SHOWERHEAD	
Policy Number: Effective Date:		Superseding Policy
Approved By: Title		
Objective:	To provide guests with clean and hygienic shower massage - specification.	pulsating shower head as per designed

Procedures:

- Should have an outer control bezel to set the intensity of water spray in any of 3 positions:

　1a. Concentrated full shower spray that cleanses and refreshens.

　2b. A gentle but invigorating massage to ease stress and tension plus a soothing spray to rinse and refresh.

　2c. A brisk, stimulating massage to work out after exercise soreness and specific tension spots.

- A ll flow regulator device must comply with mandatory water conservation measures.

- A rubber filter screen has to be placed inside the pivot ball joint and should be cleaned at least once a year or whenever you notice a drop in water pressure.

- Ideal shower head should consist of water saving restrictor, chrome plated base cone, exit plates create multiple spray patterns, inner power chamber directs water to spray plates, outer power chamber channels water flow to turbine, high speed turbine creates pulsating action, outer control bezel selects shower modes, and front spray cup creates wide pattern full spray shower.

5.5

Brands recommended: Moen and Kohler

Deviations:

5.6

Subject	
	LAUNDRY LINT CLEANING

Policy Number:	Superseding Policy
Effective Date:	

Approved By:
Title

Objective:

To eliminate the accumulation of dry, highly combustible lint on laundry machines and extract ducts.

Procedures:

3. **Daily**

   Cleaning of accumulated lint from inside of all equipment.
   Cleaning of accumulated lint from the outside of equipment, ducts and surrounding areas.
   It is mandatory for Lint Collecting Equipment:
   Empty the lint bag of lint collector (filler) regularly. This should be done once the bag is three quarters full. This has to be inspected daily by the Laundry Department, a report to be forwarded to the Engineering.

   Monthly

   Clean the filter with spray nozzle or flushing with water.
   Hose down the interior of the lint collector.

   Quarterly

   Check the exhaust fan for any build up or lint or other foreign particles. Internal cleaning of the duct.

5.6

4. Annual Cleaning

•Inspection and cleaning of the vertical and horizontal risers to be carried out.

Deviations:
Requires written approval from the RVP.

5.7

Subject	**FIRE ALARM & EMERGENCY PROCEDURES**	
Policy Number: Effective Date:		Superseding Policy
Approved By: Title		
Objective:		
To serve as guidelines in ensuring proper Fire Alarm and Emergency procedures are adhered to.		
Procedures: **Please see attached**		
Deviations: Requires written approval from the RVP		

5.8

| Subject | **INFRARED THERMOGRAPHIC SURVEY** |

| Policy Number: | Superseding Policy |
| Effective Date: | |

Approved By:
Title

Objective:

To know and prevent well in advance any overheating of cables/bus, bar/wire termination/bearing ends/bearing journal/any moving parts and other electrical and mechanical installation. To know of any points eventually which can cause short circuiting/fire/damage/breakdown. The survey is used for predictive maintenance saving down time and improving operating profits.

Procedures:

    To be carried out and on peak times.
    Contract the internationally recognized thermographic consultant with the latest imaging thermographic camera Carry out thermographic imaging on all electrical equipment.

    Record all imaging

    Carry out at least once a year
    Send report to Area Director of Engineering

    Refer - Annex I for conclusion of report.

Deviations:
Requires written approval from the RVP

5.8

Recommended:

ANNEX I
Thermographic Survey

Assessment of Seriousness

As a general rule for determining the condition of electrical equipment, any component which is 5°C or more warmer than adjacent components is considered as needing attention. The larger the temperature difference, the more serious the problem. In most cases the load on the equipment is not exactly known and different loads may account for smaller temperature differences. The following tables give a brief on temperature differentials and their required actions.

Low Voltage Systems

TEMPERATURE	ACTION	LEVEL
0° TO 10°C	Repair as scheduling permits	A
10° to 20°C	Priority repair schedule	B
20° to 30°C	Repair as soon as possible	C
Over 30°C	Repair immediately	D

High Voltage Systems

TEMPERATURE RISE	ACTION
Under 30°C	Repair as scheduling permits
30° to 50°C	Repair within 30 days
50° to 75°C	Repair Immediately

These are temperature rises above ambient or above another similar component. In most case, absolute temperatures are not so important, as they will depend upon ambient temperatures. The expected ambient temperatures should be taken into account when specifying these components.

Note that Infrared scanning can be inspected only with sufficient or maximum loads. Even serious faults cannot be detected if there is little or no current flowing.

Motors also should be included in the Infrared scanning inspection. Maximum heat generation takes place in the windings. As a general rule, the temperature on winding should not be more than 40°C above ambient. Bearing housing which is warmer than the motor body is 1 <&.9 considered to be an anomaly. The larger the difference the more serious the problem.

Subject	**KITCHEN EXTRACTOR HOOD & DUCT CLEANING**

Policy Number:	Superseding Policy
Effective Date:	

Approved by:
Title

Objective:

To eliminate grease collection from the hood and duct which is a fire hazard.

Procedures:

4. **Daily**

   Filters to be removed, degreased and cleaned.
   Hoods and the grease trap to be cleaned.

9. **Weekly**

   The Stewarding Department to prepare a checklist to be issued to the Engineering Department on a weekly basis. Standard format of the checklist is attached.
   Automatic/manual chemical degreasing of the system to be activated for the hoods. If not, hoods to be thoroughly cleaned with high pressure steam.
   Engineering Department to check the working condition of the automatic cleaning system regularly.

15. **Annual**

    Service of a specialized contractor to be hired to carry out the following. Complete
    r)   cleaning of all horizontal ducts and the vertical riser.
    s)   Smaller branches to be dismantled and cleaned. Use
)   of eco-friendly chemicals for degreasing.
    t)

5.9

a) Manual inspection doors should be provided every 6 meters straight and near smaller branches.
b) If possible, video camera to be used to assess the condition of the ducts.

Deviations :
Requires written approval from the RVP

SAMPLE
WEEKLY CHECKLIST FOR CLEANING OF KITCHEN HOOD FILTERS

WEEK NO.	MONTH	YEAR
SN		
1		
2		
3		
4		
5		
6		
7		
8		
9		

Comments:

Checked by Engineering Technician: **Signature**   Date _ _ _ _ _ _ _ _ _ _ _

Signed by the Director & Engineering

www.ingramcontent.com/pod-product-compliance
Lightning Source LLC
Chambersburg PA
CBHW052357220526
45465CB00003BB/1148